Discover Your
Destiny

"Eye hath not seen, nor ear heard,
neither have entered into the heart of man,
the things which God hath prepared
for them that love Him."
—1 Corinthians 2:9

Cary Schmidt

Striving Together Publications
4020 E. Lancaster Blvd.
Lancaster, CA 93535
800.201.7748

Cover design by Cary Schmidt and Stephen Houk

Layout by Craig Parker

Editing, proofreading, and assistance by
Amanda Michael and Kayla Nelson

ISBN 1-59894-000-7

Printed in the United States of America

Contents

dedication

This Sunday school curriculum is dedicated to the many graduates of the Lancaster Baptist student ministry who have taken these principles, put them to practice in their lives, and are reaping the fruit of young lives well-lived for God's glory! May God grant you wisdom and the passion to continue pursuing the perfect will of God throughout all of your days!

introduction

Teacher's Edition Introduction
Before We Get Started
About this material…

Discover Your Destiny is a teaching curriculum that is specifically designed for young adults between the ages of sixteen and twenty-four. This curriculum focuses on giving young adults the biblical principles they need to make right decisions. The primary goal of this material is to help young people understand the importance of finding and living within God's perfect will for their lives. These lessons are designed to give a road map that will help a young adult make decisions based upon the Word of God and the will of God.

For the past decade, this material has been presented to the juniors and seniors in the student ministry of the Lancaster Baptist Church. The students have received it with zeal and have applied it with commitment. The results over the past ten years have been exciting to see. Many young people have expressed that this material was life changing and that it truly put them on a right decision-making track.

The potential of you teaching this material well and your students receiving it could be generational in its impact! It is imperative that you as the teacher seek God's power and divine touch upon this series of lessons. The things you say, the verses you share, and the principles you discover will truly change the destiny of those you teach, as well as the destiny of those they influence in the future.

As the teacher, whether or not the students grasp the importance of these truths will greatly depend upon your personal commitment to Christ, your excitement level in teaching, and your passionate heart for making a difference in their lives. It is entirely possible to teach the right thing the wrong way. For this reason, I urge you to seek God's power and to completely lose yourself to the communication process. Be excited, be well prepared, and be acutely in tune with applying these principles to young lives. Your excitement for these truths will be contagious, and your students will embrace the passion with which you communicate.

Here are some guidelines and suggestions for teaching this material more effectively:

Take your time

There are seventeen lessons in this series, but in its original presentation in our student ministry, it usually takes twenty-four to twenty-six weeks to complete. This allows time for personal application, review, and even discussion.

Review often

It has been said that repetition is the key to learning, and this is especially true with young people. If your class is like mine, about two-thirds of the teenagers in your youth group probably suffer from ADD or some similar affliction— especially on Sunday mornings! It is no secret that teenagers are brain dead on Sunday mornings, therefore I urge you to review this material each week. Each lesson builds on the one before, and it's important that they remember all of the principles in one context. It's not uncommon for 30 to 50 percent of my lesson time to be review of the past weeks' material.

Be interactive

Get the teens involved! This is imperative. You must get their brains and their intellectual reasoning engaged with the truth. One of the easiest and simplest ways to do this is to ask questions and to get feedback from the class. There will be times throughout the lessons that you'll be encouraged to do this. Also, any time you can, physically involve the teens in illustrating a truth. It will stay with them much longer. This can be done easily and humorously with role-playing and other interactive ideas. Make sure that you lead the teens in a two-way interactive learning process as you explore these principles.

Be dynamic

At the most, you will have one hour a week in a Sunday school class to teach this material. Make the most of that hour by being energetic, excited, and vocally dynamic. Die to self, and think outside of the box. Get beyond yourself, and energetically confront your students with these life-changing principles.

Use creative illustrations

Ask the Lord to give you insight and wisdom in how to apply each truth. He will help you think of personal stories and other ways to illustrate important principles.

Use the companion materials

There are two companion resources that come with this series. The first is a 280-page paperback book entitled *Discover Your Destiny*. This book elaborates the principles in this series, and fills in the gaps with illustrations and applications. I encourage you as a teacher to read this book and to have your students read it as well. This will greatly strengthen your class time and give you greater opportunity for follow-up discussion. Also, take advantage of the student edition, which comes with blank outlines, Scripture reading, and other study helps. As your students work through these outlines, this will become a resource that they will refer to for years to come.

Teach this material a minimum of every two years

If you haven't noticed, teenagers grow up quickly. About a year after you teach this material, those who heard it will have graduated from your youth group, and you will have another group of young people who desperately need these truths. Make a long-term commitment to preparing young people for adulthood. God will bless your efforts in helping others live in His perfect will.

Have fun

When presented the right way, this material can be immensely enjoyable. Two or three times throughout the course of this study, I generally take an entire class period to review the material up to that point. I divide the class into two teams, and we have a simple review quiz. Sometimes we play guys against girls or eleventh grade against twelfth grade. Either way, it always ends up being a lot of fun, and it really helps the teens remember what they've learned. This is just one idea among many that will help the students have a great time while they learn life-changing truths.

Thank you for having a heart to help young people make right decisions for God. May God richly bless you as you help others discover their destiny. We would love to hear feedback on how God uses this material in the lives of your young people. Please let us know your comments by sending an email to strivingtogether@lancasterbaptist.org.

Sincerely,

Cary Schmidt

how to

How To Use This Curriculum

Listed below is the description of how this curriculum is structured and how to best use it in teaching young adults. Each lesson in this teacher's manual will include the following:

Title and Subtitle

This will always correspond to the book chapter title, as well as the student edition chapter title.

Text

This text will provide a starting point and key Scripture references upon which the lesson will be built.

Lesson Aim

This short statement will articulate the key purpose and goals of the particular lesson.

Teaching Outline

This outline will give you an overview of each lesson in its entirety. The outlines are not alliterated and often vary in structure from lesson to lesson. Each outline reflects the blanks in the student workbook.

Lesson Content

This section will provide the teacher with the basic content of each lesson. Throughout the content section, you will occasionally find teaching tips, which will help you specifically apply or communicate a key principle.

You will also find many scriptural cross-references throughout the content portion of each lesson. It is suggested that you have students turn to these passages of Scripture and actually read them out loud as you work through your lesson.

The original content of the book *Discover Your Destiny* was not written by a strict outline, therefore the flow of the context will sometimes vary slightly from the flow of the outline. It is suggested that you follow the outline flow in teaching because this matches the student workbook.

Review Points for the Next Week

At the conclusion of each lesson, you will find a list of discussion questions to review the next week. These are provided as discussion starters for the beginning of the next week's lesson, and are reflected as study questions in the student workbook.

Lesson Notes

Each lesson will have a section of blank lines provided for you to make your own notes or application thoughts.

It's Not Easy Being Dysfunctional

Starting the Journey from a Point of Need

Text

"Remember now thy Creator in the days of thy youth, while the evil days come not, nor the years draw nigh, when thou shalt say, I have no pleasure in them;"—Ecclesiastes 12:1

Lesson Aim

This lesson is introductory and is designed to create an awareness of vulnerability. Teenagers must know how dependent they should be on God as they enter an adult life for which they are not prepared.

Teaching Outline

I. Congratulations, you're great at being a kid!
   A. You hate to be thought of as a kid.
   B. You long to be thought of as an adult.
   C. You crave independence.
   D. You are probably excited about the future.

II. Congratulations, you're not ready to be an adult!
   A. You haven't lived adult life before.
   B. You haven't made adult decisions before.
   C. You could spend the next thirty years learning lessons the hard way.

III. Congratulations, you need God!
   A. We are all dysfunctional.
   B. We cannot survive this journey without God.
   C. We must admit and accept our dependence upon God and others. (James 4:6; Proverbs 8:17; Hebrews 11:6)
   D. We must live life by God's rules.

one

Lesson One
It's Not Easy Being Dysfunctional
Starting the Journey from a Point of Need

I. Congratulations, you're great at being a kid!

As a young person, you too are dysfunctional. Unless you're just way ahead of your time, you probably still enjoy a good Scooby-Doo cartoon and a pop tart just like I do. As a young adult, you know just enough about life to be dangerous! Everybody wants to feel like they've arrived when they turn eighteen. You can vote; you can drive; you can stay out late…the world says, "You are now grown up!"

Just don't get too hooked on that line yet. Reality is, you're just now getting really good at being a kid! Think about it! What do you really know about buying a home, rearing children, getting a good interest rate on a new car, developing a career, or even keeping a marriage together? Honestly…probably very little. You probably know just enough about these things to get yourself into trouble, but this is the stuff of adult life. This is the stuff you're going to be doing sooner than later...and NOW is the time to get ready.

Now, being a kid on the other hand...you're probably pretty good at that. You could whip out a quick one-page book report in no time flat. If some fourth-grader needed help in math, you're "the man!" You've got all kinds of answers for things like: "How to Clean Your Room So Mom Will Never Know" or "How to Cope With an Insane Substitute Teacher" or "How to Use Pain to Dominate a Younger Sibling" or even "How to Pass Geometry." This stuff is easy for you. You've been there and done that.

The problem comes when somehow we reason that all of this has made us ready for adult life. Somehow we assume that we've passed the tests, we've gained the credentials, and we're ready to sail. We think having been successful kids makes us ready to be successful adults, but nothing could be farther from the truth!

On top of that you're probably excited about the future. You've got ideas. You've got plans and dreams. You know where you want to go, what you want to become, and how your life will be lived. You are "the man!" (or woman). You're ready to charge into adult life, and you probably even get irritated when people try to give you advice for which you did not ask. High school or college has prepared you for the land of adulthood, and you are convinced that your destiny awaits...you're ready to seize the moment!

II. Congratulations, you're not ready to be an adult!

Passing the tests of childhood doesn't mean you're ready for the major leagues. In fact, being so self-confident is one of the surest ways to fall flat on your face. Truth is, the world is full of people who are great at being kids, but they make terrible adults. They are immature, insecure, and they make decisions that ruin lives. They look happy on the outside, but they are miserable on the inside, and their future will get worse.

The fact of the matter is you have come a long way, and you didn't get here by being totally stupid. Sure you've done a good job up to this point. You've passed some grades, figured out how to please your parents, turned in a few science projects, and if you're really good, maybe you've even flipped a few burgers and assembled a few Happy Meals. So, we'll give you some credit from the start...but probably not as much as you would give yourself. It took a lot to get where you are, but it's going to take a lot more to get to your destiny.

One of the definitions for the word *dysfunctional* is "unable to function normally as a result of disease or impairment." The disease is sin—specifically pride—and the impairment is immaturity, and we all have it. We're all facing life with horrific spiritual deficiencies, which makes us all dependent upon God, His grace, and His awesome leading in our lives.

The difference between you and someone forty years older than you is that #1—you haven't ruined your life yet (You may think you have, but believe me, you haven't...there's hope). And #2—you haven't lived long enough to learn life's biggest lessons the hard way. Most people spend the better part of several decades realizing how little they really know about life...and most of them NEVER realize how much they need God. As we go through this study hopefully you will avoid those mistakes. There's no reason to forfeit your future "learning the hard way!"

It will be a wonderful day in your life when you accept the fact that you are not ready for the adult life that you are about to enter. The decisions you must make are bigger than you. You haven't been down this road before. Why is it so hard for young adults to see and admit that? You will finally be on the road to true success when you can admit to yourself and others that you do not have the wisdom and the knowledge to survive alone. For only then can you truly become the recipient of all God wants to give you.

III. Congratulations, you need God!

God's best for your future starts at a point of need not a point of strength. If you view yourself in a position of strength, if you have the "I'm my own man" disease, you are in for some serious disappointment. People with this disease spend a large portion of their life figuring out that they are not really as great as they think.

If, on the other hand, you view yourself in a position of need, if you see the decisions you face through the eyes of humility and sincerity, then you will be driven to the Lord, to His Word, and to His guidance through godly adults that you trust. If you are approaching your future with an uncertain mixture of excitement, hesitation, fear, and anticipation, then you are certainly approaching a position of blessing. If you know that you need God, then He will be found, and His blessings will follow. God tells us that He *"resisteth the proud but giveth grace to the humble"* (James 4:6). Also, He promises in Proverbs 8:17, *"I love them that love me; and those that seek me early shall find me."*

Lest you think I'm picking on you…I'm in the same boat! Though I'm a little farther down the road than you are, I still face an uncertain future every day! I still find myself totally and utterly dependent upon God's leading day by day so that I may continue discovering my own destiny. This is how it will be the rest of my life!

I've seen too many friends and too many students graduate from high school and ruin their lives with bad decisions. I'm convinced that there's a better way, and in these lessons I hope to kick-start you into the wonderful journey of discovering God's best for your future. I hope to burn into your own heart a passion to settle for nothing less than God's best!

Simply put, there is no other true life. There are substitutes. There are second-hand copies. But you have only one destiny designed by God and only one life with which to discover it. You can't rewind. You can't start over. You'll never pass "go." One chance is all you get. Who ever heard of a game where you only get one turn? Welcome to real life. These are God's rules. You go around one time, then you stand before Him to give an account. You cannot see the future; you cannot cheat. You cannot really be sure of anything but Him. You and only you will give account for you. You cannot blame anyone or anything else for mistakes or failures. You will be given full and unrestricted access to God, but only by faith. You cannot see Him or audibly hear Him. You will be given His Word and His promises. You will be subject to His laws, yet given the free will to rebel against a select number of them. In the end, you will face eternity. You will answer only to God, and you will live somewhere forever. There are no time-outs, and you never know for sure when the game will end. As you are learning the game, it has already started, and it could end at any moment. You'll know that the game is over when you are flat on your face before Jesus Christ. Your turn will be first, you are the only player in your "race," and it's always your turn. On your mark; get set; go!

Life is awesome! It really is great to be an adult and experience God's gifts day by day, but there are many risks. There are many ways to miss God's awesome plans for your future. In these lessons, we will journey through a process of spiritual growth and decision-making that will help you step by step through the decisions ahead.

They work! These principles work because they are from the Bible. The principles that I will share with you come directly from God's Word—the Bible. The Bible is a supernatural Book with a supernatural message from God. It is His Guidebook for your life. It is absolutely true. Thousands have tried to disprove it, but failed. There are dozens of proofs that I could share with you to prove that the Bible is true and trustworthy. If you're not "there" in your heart, I would challenge you to start studying the issue and settle it soon. You will fail in life if you live without the guidance of God's Word; however, if you will apply the principles that we will discover, you'll be guaranteed, with God's help, that every major decision in your future will be made correctly.

Open up your heart and decide that you want to learn as much as you can about the journey ahead. I wish I could tell you how awesome it's going to be. I can't see your future any more than you can. The rules don't allow that. You just have to choose to trust God and discover His good plan one day at a time as He unveils it to you.

Let me warn you now, this is heavy stuff! It's HUGE! This stuff affects generations, and I refuse to go easy on you. I'm going to "tell it like it is"…like it or not. I'm sure, at some points in this series, you won't like what you hear, but I promise you that I'll only share truths that are supported from God's Word. So, your argument is with Him not me. If you could see the end from the beginning, there would be no argument. Yet, through God's Word and through the help of those who have "been there before" in a vague sort of way, we *can* see the end from the beginning.

You probably have a lot of questions about your future. Questions like "What is God's will?" "How can I find it?" "How will I know for sure?" "What does it mean to be called into ministry?" "How do I know if I'm called?" "When will I know?" On and on the list could go. I hope you're hungry for answers, because that's a great start. You're going to love the journey!

"...he is a rewarder of them that diligently seek him."
—Hebrews 11:6b

Discussion Questions

1. When should you start getting ready for adulthood?
2. What does it mean to be "dysfunctional"?
3. Before God can lead you into his best blessings for your future, what do you need to realize and accept?
4. When it comes to destiny, what are God's "rules"?
5. In what areas of life do you tend to think you're more ready for than you really are?
6. Why do some people get irritated when others try to give them advice about adulthood?
7. How can admitting that you're dysfunctional and that you need God help you today?
8. List three things you can do this week to show God that you are depending upon Him.

Memory Verse

"I love them that love me; and those that seek me early shall find me."—Proverbs 8:17

Lesson Notes

_____

_____

_____

_____

_____

_____

_____

_____

_____

_____

_____

_____

_____

_____

_____

_____

_____

_____

_____

_____

_____

_____

_____

Lesson Notes

_____

_____

_____

_____

_____

_____

_____

_____

_____

_____

_____

_____

_____

_____

_____

_____

_____

_____

_____

_____

_____

_____

_____

Welcome to the "Mistake Zone"

The Ten Most Dangerous Years of Everyone's Life

Text

"Remember now thy Creator in the days of thy youth, while the evil days come not, nor the years draw nigh, when thou shalt say, I have no pleasure in them;"—Ecclesiastes 12:1

"Blessed is the man that walketh not in the counsel of the ungodly, nor standeth in the way of sinners, nor sitteth in the seat of the scornful. But his delight is in the law of the LORD; and in his law doth he meditate day and night. And he shall be like a tree planted by the rivers of water, that bringeth forth his fruit in his season; his leaf also shall not wither; and whatsoever he doeth shall prosper."—Psalm 1:1–3

"The steps of a good man are ordered by the LORD: and he delighteth in his way."—Psalm 37:23

"A thousand shall fall at thy side, and ten thousand at thy right hand; but it shall not come nigh thee. Only with thine eyes shalt thou behold and see the reward of the wicked. Because thou hast made the LORD, which is my refuge, even the most High, thy habitation;"—Psalm 91:7–9

Lesson Aim

The purpose of this lesson is to help teenagers grasp the enormous magnitude of the life-changing decisions they will be required to make in the next ten years.

Teaching Outline

   I. Introducing the "Mistake Zone"

      A. The "Mistake Zone" encompasses ages seventeen to twenty-seven.

      B. The "Mistake Zone" is when life's biggest decisions will be made.

      C. The "Mistake Zone" is where life's biggest mistakes will be made.

      D. These mistakes have life-long implications.

  II. Understanding "Mistake Zone" Decisions

      A. These decisions have life-long consequences.

      B. You cannot see the outcome of these decisions until after they are made.

      C. None of these decisions will happen by luck, happenstance, or default.

two

Lesson Two
Welcome to the "Mistake Zone"
The Ten Most Dangerous Years of Everyone's Life

You're at the dawning of adulthood with nothing but promise on the horizon and a world of choices staring you in the face.

You are now in the "Mistake Zone." Look around and see the casualties.

I. Introducing the "Mistake Zone"

You are about to enter a dimension of time and space. It's a dimension where people do things on their own with little regard for the consequences, a dimension where people think they know everything, and rarely admit that they don't. It's a dimension where decisions are made that determine the outcome of the rest of your life and where generations are impacted by the choices you will make. You are about to enter the "Mistake Zone."

The "Mistake Zone" is a period of time between childhood and sanity where most people do stupid things. The "Mistake Zone" can be roughly estimated to be between the ages of seventeen and twenty-seven, give or take a few years either way depending on your individual life. It's the time of life when almost all of your biggest decisions will be made, yet it's the time of life when you are the very least equipped to make those decisions. Scary? You bet. Can you avoid it? Absolutely not.

If you are seventeen years or older, you're there now! So stop! Before you make another major decision, take a look at the landscape of people who have been through the "Mistake Zone". You'll find casualties no matter where you look. You'll find unwanted pregnancies, abortions, and sexually-transmitted diseases. You'll find alcoholism, drug abuse, and chain-smokers. You'll find divorce, custody battles, and broken lives. You'll find relational abuse, substance abuse, and sexual abuse. You'll find bad credit, lost jobs, and bad investments. You'll find school drop-outs, down-and-outers, and even up-and-outers. You'll find casualties on skid row and at the Ritz Carlton. No one is exempt from the pain and scars of the "Mistake Zone". Not even you.

You're not exempt from any of these things, and neither am I. The "Mistake Zone" is no respecter of persons. Your background or pedigree won't buy you an advantage. Everyone must travel through the "Mistake Zone," but not everyone has to make life-altering bad decisions. Sure, we all make mistakes; no one is perfect, but you can make it through the "Mistake Zone" without ruining your life. You don't have to be a casualty.

One more thought, making it through the "Mistake Zone" doesn't mean you're exempt from future mistakes. I'm not off the hook, and neither are your parents. It just means that you made it through a potential mine field of bad decisions. There will be plenty of chances to blow it beyond twenty-seven, but for those who do make hugely bad decisions, most of them are made in the "Mistake Zone."

Teaching Tip:

Rather than creating this list as a teacher, make this list an interactive part of class. Introduce the lesson, and then ask the students to come up with their own suggestions of the decisions they will face in the next ten years. Start writing the decisions on the board, and you will be surprised how similar their answers are to this list. This makes for a great interactive class time!

II. Understanding "Mistake Zone" decisions

So let's think about it. Here's a list of decisions that you will probably make between the ages of seventeen and twenty-seven.

- College
- Dating
- First Job
- First Car
- Friends
- Career Field
- Marriage
- Career Location
- Living Quarters
- Children and Family
- Church
- Personal Walk with Christ
- Life's Purpose and Mission
- Financial Values

That's a pretty long list. Take a look at it again and remind yourself that most of these decisions will be made over the next ten years in your life. These things are *gigantic!* These are mammoth decisions that must be made, and you're just now starting adulthood with no way of really knowing for sure which way is right for your future. Seems unfair doesn't it? Seems somehow out of whack! God intentionally places these huge, beefy decisions on your plate, and you've just barely started "teething!" He knows you're not ready, but He has put you here anyway. Makes you wonder what kind of strange sense of humor He really has doesn't it?

That's not it at all. He's put you here so that you will feel very small in the face of such overwhelming circumstances. He wants you to feel that the odds are terribly against you so that you will know without any doubt how desperately you need Him. "Strange" would be if God put you here with no access to Himself or His guidance. No…this is just a faith-based relationship. We'll get to that later.

Seems crazy that so many trudge right on through with no thought of God at all. You know why? They've been taught that life is some sort of cosmic mistake, and that they are nothing more than a genetic, evolutionary freak of nature…which means nothing matters anyway. Friend, that's not the case, and we'll talk about that later as well.

For now, let's look more closely at these decisions. You're not quite "freaked out" enough yet for my liking, but you soon will be.

"Remember now thy Creator in the days of thy youth, while the evil days come not, nor the years draw nigh, when thou shalt say, I have no pleasure in them;"—Ecclesiastes 12:1

Discussion Questions

1. What is the "Mistake Zone"?
2. List several major decisions you will make in the "Mistake Zone."
3. What are some results of making wrong decisions in the "Mistake Zone"?
4. What is God's promise to you during these crucial years of decision-making?
5. Why do you think God allows you to go through the "Mistake Zone"?
6. Why are you not qualified to make these decisions on your own?
7. What kinds of thought patterns, habits, or characteristics can lead someone to making a wrong decision? What can you do to keep yourself from going this same direction?
8. What is the most important principle for you to remember as you go through the "Mistake Zone"?

Memory Verse

"Lead me, O LORD, in thy righteousness because of mine enemies; make thy way straight before my face."—Psalm 5:8

Lesson Notes

_____

_____

_____

_____

_____

_____

_____

_____

_____

_____

_____

_____

_____

_____

_____

_____

_____

_____

_____

_____

_____

_____

In the Heart of the "Mistake Zone"

Understanding the Risk

Text

"Behold, God is my salvation; I will trust, and not be afraid: for the LORD JEHOVAH is my strength and my song; he also is become my salvation."—Isaiah 12:2

"For God hath not given us the spirit of fear; but of power, and of love, and of a sound mind."—2 Timothy 1:7

Lesson Aim

The purpose of this lesson is to take a closer look at the "Mistake Zone" and to spend time discussing each of the decisions in detail. This will help the students grasp the importance of the risk and the importance of making these decisions right, the first time around.

This lesson is really designed to raise as many questions as possible. This will set the stage for answering these questions God's way in the coming weeks. If taught correctly, these lessons should leave your students feeling like they're hanging by a thread—on the edge of making the most critical decisions of their lives.

Teaching Outline

I. Which college will you go to?
    A. It will determine your life course.
    B. It will probably determine your life spouse.
    C. It will determine your friends.

II. Who will you date? (Amos 3:3; 2 Corinthians 6:14)
  A. Who you date will determine your testimony.
  B. Who you date will determine who you marry.
  C. Who you date will greatly impact the condition of your spiritual heart.

III. What will your first job be?
  A. Your first job will determine God's true priority in your life.
  B. Your first job could help you trust God.
  C. Your first job will reveal your true spiritual character.

IV. What will you drive?
  A. How you buy a car will reveal your intelligence.
  B. How you drive a car will reveal your maturity.
  C. How you care for a car will reveal your character.

V. Who will be your friends?
  A. You will become like your friends.
  B. People will judge you by your friends. (1 Samuel 16:7)
  C. Your friends will influence every part of your life.

VI. What career field will you choose?
  A. The question is not "what do you want to do?"
  B. The question is "what did God create you to do?"
  C. God's purpose is the only thing that will truly make you happy.

VII. Who will you marry?
  A. A great marriage is not easy.
  B. A great marriage is worth fighting for.
  C. Most marriages without God fail.
  D. Only God can give you a great marriage.

VIII. Where will you locate in your career?
  A. This will determine where you live.
  B. This will determine where your family grows up.
  C. This will determine the entire spiritual future of your family.

IX. What will you live in?
  A. Will you rent or purchase?
  B. What does it take to buy or rent a living space?
  C. How will you know you're making the right decision?

X. When will you have children and a family?
  A. When will you have kids?
  B. How many will you have?
  C. How will you raise them?
  D. What will their futures be like?

XI. What church will you go to?
  A. Will you live for God faithfully?
  B. What kind of church will you attend?
  C. Will you lead your family to love God?

XII. Will you maintain a personal walk with Christ?
  A. Will you stay faithful to God?
  B. Will you lead others to stay faithful to God?

XIII. What is your life's purpose and mission?
  A. Will you live for money?
  B. Will you live for pleasure?
  C. Will you live for possessions?
  D. Will you live for God alone and let Him add all these things to you?

XIV. What financial values will you live by?
   A. Will you steward your money by
       God's principles?
   B. Will you honor God?
   C. Will God be able to trust you with more?

three

Lesson Three
In the Heart of the "Mistake Zone"
Understanding the Risk

Most people are resigned to the fact that you just have to go through this "Mistake Zone," and you'll learn the hard way. Of course, most young adults "box themselves in" by refusing to hear any advice from those who care. So, they are condemned to "learn the hard way."

Honestly, adult life is a big enough adjustment, and there's no sense in carrying baggage that you don't have to carry. So, let's examine each of the major decisions you'll face in the upcoming years and try to grasp just what you're up against.

I. Which college will you go to?

If you're in high school this is probably your first major decision to conquer. Which one? What kind? Where? The college you choose will most likely lead to the person you marry, the career field you pursue, and the friends you keep. This will determine where you live, what you will do with the rest of your life, who you become like, and whose children you have. This will determine who your grandkids will be and who their kids will be…and so on. Whoa…big stuff. This is definitely a major decision that you want to get right!

II. Who will you date?

What kind of person will you date? If "looks" are your primary criteria, you're headed for a world of misery. (Although, I wouldn't go so far as to tell you to marry someone ugly.) Believe me, when you meet God's match for you, you'll think this is the best looking person on the planet. That's an easy one for God.

What guidelines will you follow in your dating life? Who will you give an account to? How will you keep from ruining your testimony? Will your dating life reflect Christ and help you become a better Christian? These questions will formulate the basis for choosing a spouse, a life's mate. This is huge!

Will you date a non-Christian? Other than the fact that it's clear in the Bible, it's just common sense. If God is real and your faith is real, then your family must be founded upon eternal values. God's Word is the blueprint for the family and the glue that holds it together. If you don't at least have true faith in common, you're headed for sure disaster. God says in Amos 3:3, *"Can two walk together, except they be agreed?"* And 2 Corinthians 6:14 says, *"Be ye not unequally yoked together with unbelievers: for what fellowship hath righteousness with unrighteousness? and what communion hath light with darkness?"* By the way, don't fall for the trap that you can date this person and win him to Christ. Win him to Christ, see him discipled to faithfulness…*then* date him. Very few people succeed with dating as an outreach. It's never right to do wrong to do right.

III. What will your first job be?

Where will you work through young adulthood? Most people get some small job in high school that causes them to face a lot of life-shaping questions. Will you work on Sundays? So many young adults get so infatuated with getting their first few paychecks that they will kiss Sunday church goodbye for the first minimum wage offer that comes along. They love the sound of being able to say "I have to work." There's something very adult-ish about that.

So, as a side note, choose now, before you get your job, to stay in church regardless. Starter jobs are easy to find. Good workers are hard to find, and God will provide better for you than you will for yourself. Keep Him first, and watch Him work it out. If you have a job now that requires you to miss Sunday church, talk to your manager, get your parent's and pastor's advice…and even consider putting in your notice if you have to. Put God to the test, and let Him prove Himself to you. Stepping out in faith is easier now than it will ever be, and you'll need the valuable foundation of faith for bigger decisions in your future. In other words, learn to trust God with $6.50 an hour, and it will be easier to trust Him with $80,000 a year, when your kids will be watching you.

People who refuse to trust God when they are young never develop the foundation of faith that they need when bigger storms and harder tests come their way. Remember David and Goliath? David trusted God with the bear and the lion, which made it easier for him to trust God with Goliath. The same principle will work for you.

On your job, will you stand for right? Will you laugh at dirty jokes and accept invitations to wild parties? Will you be a credible testimony for Christ, or will you quietly hide your Christianity for the myth of acceptance? What will you do for money? What will you do with your money? These values and more start coming into focus with the starting of your first job and will determine a wide variety of details about your adult life.

IV. What will you drive?

Will you have a car soon? Will God provide for you to buy one? What kind? How much should you pay? What interest rate will you get, and how will you know if you got a good deal? How much money will you need to keep it running? Can you pay insurance? How will you treat it? How will you drive it? On and on the list goes.

The world is quietly awaiting your answer. By it they will determine what kind of person you are. If you drive recklessly, people will rightly judge you as immature and unprepared for real responsibility. People will tell their kids they can't hang out with you. You'll be a statistic in someone's message or an illustration in some parental lecture of "who not to be like." Is that what you want? Really? Do you want people to look at you and say, "Stay away from that kid?" Is that worth a few "donuts" in the church parking lot or a "drag race" on the edge of town? No. But, it happens all the time in the "Mistake Zone."

V. Who will be your friends?

Who will you hang around and spend time with? Who will
you be like and be associated with? What kind of person
do you want to become? Who will you decide you want
acceptance from and why even care about acceptance? These
issues are very significant. People will mentally judge you
based upon the people you spend time with. "Not fair," you
might think. Wrong. It's completely fair, and you do the
same thing. You're human and God makes it clear that *"man
looketh on the outward appearance"* (1 Samuel 16:7).

"Yeah, but God looks at the heart," you argue.

Yeah…but man looks at the outward appearance. People
only have what you give them to formulate their opinion of
you. If it's a bad opinion, it's probably your fault. Don't go
blaming everyone else for misjudging you. Take a look in the
mirror and study what you're giving them to work with. Start
with a good look at your friends.

The fact is people are right in judging you this way
because you will become like the people you spend time with.
So rather than looking for who's cool, who's "in," or who's
acceptable, start looking for who you want to be like and be
associated with and make them your friends. This decision
determines who you will be like which again has profound
effects on everything else…who will marry you, who will
hire you, who will help you in time of trial…on and on.

VI. What career field will you choose?

What will you spend your life doing? There are many noble
things to do with your life. Ministry is good. Faithful
Christians in secular fields are vital also. The question is
not "what do you want to do?" As we'll see later, that can

be a dangerous way to think. The question is—what is your destiny? What were you made to do? What fulfills your eternal purpose for being on this planet? When you answer that question, you will be truly happy.

Chances are you know what you want. Scary thing is you may or may not be right. I mean, what you think you want may be absolutely wrong for your destiny. In which case, you won't know it until a few years down the road… probably after you exit the "Mistake Zone." So, you will have to make a choice, but you have no real way of knowing that what you want is what God wants. Sounds too bizarre for reality, but it's true. The world is full of elderly people who never really found their purpose for being alive. You don't have to become one of them.

VII. Who will you marry?

Who will you marry? What kind of person will you marry? I mean, beyond "pretty" or "handsome." Come on, go a little deeper than that. How will you know this person is emotionally stable? How will you be guaranteed you won't end up deserted, cheated on, or left hanging out to dry? Thousands of couples every year, who once stood at a wedding altar madly in love, stand in a living room beating each other's brains out or stand in a courtroom fighting over cars and kids. People who once dreamed of living in love for the rest of their lives now live in hate. How can that happen? What makes you exempt? No one thinks it will happen to them.

Your marriage will not be perfect. At best it will be a solid relationship that forges through trials to become a refined lifetime love. That's at best. No marriage is easy, and no marriage just falls into perfect place. Happy marriages and lifetime loves are discovered through years of commitment and personal change. But happy marriages are worth fighting for. They are always happier after the forging process than they were before it. The whole relationship gets better over time…but how will you know for sure that you've got someone committed to loving that intensely?

How will this person treat your children? How will they respond when you do something stupid? How will they spend money or keep the house? What will it take to really make them "ticked off." Just what does this person do when he or she is "ticked off"? What will he or she want to do with the rest of your life?

All of these questions are huge, and most of them cannot be answered for certain until after you're married! Isn't that great news! You'll fall in love and get married, and then you'll start to really get to know the person you married. About ten years later, if you are one of the few that make it, you'll feel like you're starting to get to know your spouse, and you'll thank God you followed Him…or you'll wish you had.

Now don't freak out and say something stupid like "I'm never getting married." If that's God's plan, then fine…but in reality, marriage is awesome. It's just not what pop-culture would lead you to believe. It's something much different and actually much better.

The great part is God has a plan for making sure you get the right person! We'll talk about that later. So for now, don't sweat it.

VIII. Where will you locate in your career?

Where will you live? What company or organization will you work for? Will the job be solid? Will the ministry "stay afloat"? Where will your family grow up? Who will your kids be friends with? What church will you attend? What community will you live in? Who will baby-sit your kids and influence your family? What school will you send your kids to? These questions have enormous implications on many parts of your future and family. You must get it right. You must believe there is a God-ordained purpose and plan to it all that must be discovered.

IX. What will you live in?

What kind of place will you put your family in? How much will you have to pay? When will you purchase a home, if ever? How? What does it take to get into an apartment? How do you know what is best when you've never traveled this road before?

X. When will you have children and a family?

When should you become a parent? How do you prepare for parenthood? How many children will you have? What will you teach them, and where will you take them to have fun? How will you discipline them? How will you express love to them? How will you help them avoid the mistakes you made? Can you even count the generations of people to come from your family that will know Christ or not know Him based on your decisions? Will you pray with them and read God's Word to them? Will they know God because you know Him, or will they forsake Him because you never really knew Him?

XI. What church will you go to?

Will you go since your parents won't be making you? What kind? Will you serve faithfully? Will you be what God wants you to be in your church family? Will you help to bring others to Christ in that church? Will you find a solid Bible-believing church home or will you choose a compromising, middle-of-the-road, never-leave-your-comfort-zone type of place?

XII. Will you maintain a personal walk with Christ?

Will you know Him personally and stay faithful to Him in your heart? Will your children follow your faith or leave it? Will God be a small part of your big picture, or will He be your big picture? Will God be that part of your life that you run to only when you're in trouble?

These decisions will have much to do with your own personal sanity as well as the spiritual health of your family for generations to come.

XIII. What is your life's purpose and mission?

What will be your motivation for getting out of bed every morning? Why endure the daily grind of paying the bills, feeding the family, fixing the car, and mowing the lawn? Why get up, go to work, come home, go to bed just to do it all over again every day? Will you live for money? Money makes a terrible god. Will you live for ego? No telling what you'll do then. Will you live for pleasure or fun? You'll spend your life running from one thing to the next never to be full of joy and always ending up empty and wishing you were someone else.

Will you live your life for things? That's no good…they can't love you back. Things break. Things rot. Things get stolen. Things don't last very long. Things can't go with you when you die. Things make terrible gods. Don't live for things. Use things and be thankful for them when God gives them to you. Remember that it's God that gives you richly all "things" to enjoy. But don't worship them.

What will you die with? What will be the ultimate goal of your life and reason for living? What would you like people to say about you after you're dead?

"Nobody could play basketball like that guy!"—naaa.

"Man, did she make a beautiful homecoming queen!"— wrong.

"He made a mean Big Mac when he worked at McD's"— I don't think so.

"He had the coolest boat in town!"—probably not.

"He never saw his family! What a workaholic!"—hope not.

"Who gets all his money?"—now we're in trouble.

You have to live for something. You will have a mission, whether you realize it or not. So, what will it be? Let me give you a couple of clues. It should be something that lasts forever, and it should be something that God designed you to do. We'll come back to this.

XIV. What financial values will you live by?

How much will God be able to trust you with? Will you place Him first in your life and prove it by your tithes and offerings? Will you fight with your spouse over money? What values will your kids learn about money? Will you invest money you cannot keep into an eternity that you cannot lose?

There are others that we didn't look at, and since everybody is different you'll probably face some questions that are unique to your life and destiny. Each of these questions will be answered in the few years ahead and will follow you throughout your life for better or for worse. You'll be forever linked to the outcome of the decisions you make. Inseparable, they will follow you the entire course of your life and will be irreversible.

Think of the "Mistake Zone" like a minefield, and only God knows where the mines are. He's ready to guide you through. You can run headlong through, alone if you choose. But, if you trust Him, follow Him, and seek Him, you won't get blown up. While people all around you are making wrong decisions, you can defy the odds. You don't have to be a victim of the "Mistake Zone." It's real, and it's NOW, and it's here for a while. Walk softly, stranger.

God's promise to you, if you will let Him guide you through the "minefield" of decisions, is found in Psalm 91:7–9, *"A thousand shall fall at thy side, and ten thousand at thy right hand; but it shall not come nigh thee. Only with thine eyes shalt thou behold and see the reward of the wicked. Because thou hast made the LORD, which is my refuge, even the most High, thy habitation."*

"Behold, God is my salvation; I will trust, and not be afraid: for the LORD JEHOVAH is my strength and my song; he also is become my salvation."—Isaiah 12:2

Discussion Questions

1. What will most likely be your first major decision and why is making the right decision so important?
2. Why shouldn't you date a non-Christian?
3. In what ways do friends influence you?
4. What should you look for in a future spouse?
5. Is God more important to you than a paycheck? List some ways you can protect yourself from ever replacing God with a future job.
6. Do you want your life's purpose and mission to be for money, pleasure, possessions, or God? Based on the amount of time you give to each of these in your life right now, which one are you currently living for and what can you do to move forward in the right direction?
7. List some ways that having a car can reflect well or poorly on you.
8. Based on God's promise to you in Psalm 91:7–9, what can you be sure of as you face these decisions?

Memory Verse

"Teach me to do thy will; for thou art my God: thy spirit is good; lead me into the land of uprightness."—Psalm 143:10

Lesson Notes

_____

_____

_____

_____

_____

_____

_____

_____

_____

_____

_____

_____

_____

_____

_____

_____

_____

_____

_____

_____

_____

_____

_____

_____

_____

_____

Lesson Notes

_____

_____

_____

_____

_____

_____

_____

_____

_____

_____

_____

_____

_____

_____

_____

_____

_____

_____

_____

_____

_____

_____

_____

_____

_____

Destiny—My Place in the Cosmic Cookie Mix

Understanding Time, Eternity, and Destiny

Text

"Wherefore I put thee in remembrance that thou stir up the gift of God, which is in thee by the putting on of my hands. For God hath not given us the spirit of fear; but of power, and of love, and of a sound mind. Be not thou therefore ashamed of the testimony of our Lord, nor of me his prisoner: but be thou partaker of the afflictions of the gospel according to the power of God; Who hath saved us, and called us with an holy calling, not according to our works, but according to his own purpose and grace, which was given us in Christ Jesus before the world began,"—2 Timothy 1:6–9

"Before I formed thee in the belly I knew thee; and before thou camest forth out of the womb I sanctified thee, and I ordained thee a prophet unto the nations."—Jeremiah 1:5

"For I know the thoughts that I think toward you, saith the LORD, thoughts of peace, and not of evil, to give you an expected end."—Jeremiah 29:11

Lesson Aim

The purpose of this lesson is to help the students understand God's eternal plan for their lives as conceived before the world began. This lesson will help a young person understand that they are not an accident but a masterful design of the Heavenly Father and that they have a divine mission to fulfill for eternity. This lesson is easily divided into two parts. The first part will cover Creation and evolution. The second part will begin dissecting the ideas of Eternity and Destiny.

Teaching Outline

I. The way it didn't happen
   A. Evolution is without valid evidence.
   B. The universe shows careful, deliberate, intelligent design.
   C. No evidence shows animals crossing species and producing fertile offspring.
   D. Evolution is not observable, which means it is not science.
   E. History, science, and archeology all support the biblical account of creation 100%.
   F. Evolution is a religion of blind faith; Creation is a religion of intelligent faith.
   G. The fossil record supports Creation, not evolution.

II. The way it really happened and why it matters (Psalm 19:1)
   A. God created everything.
   B. God has an eternal purpose and plan for everything He created.
   C. Your belief about Creation will determine your value system.
   D. You are not an accident.
   E. You have an eternal purpose.

III. The beginning of destiny
   A. God has an eternal purpose that's
      bigger than time. (Ephesians 1:3–12)
   B. God made you to fulfill an eternal
      purpose. (Jeremiah 1:5; Psalm 71:6; Isaiah
      49:5; Galatians 1:15; Romans 8:29)
   C. God designed your purpose before He
      created the world. (2 Timothy 1:9)

IV. Understanding destiny
   A. Your destiny is unique to you.
   B. Your destiny is awesome!
   C. You will only be happy as you fulfill your destiny.
   D. Your destiny will give you a true
      sense of divine security.
   E. Your destiny represents true success.
   F. Your destiny can be missed.
   G. Your destiny is now.
   H. Your destiny arrives from God, by
      faith, on a need-to-know basis.
   I. Your destiny is a deliberate choice.

four

Lesson Four
Destiny—My Place in the Cosmic Cookie Mix
Understanding Time, Eternity, and Destiny

I. The way it didn't happen

If you attended a public school, you've probably been sitting in a science class at some point when your teacher began talking about the origin of life. It all sounds so scientific. It goes something like this...first there was just space and gas and stuff. What kind of stuff, we're just not sure. Where the stuff came from? Well, we're just not sure about that either. We'll avoid those questions for now...(how convenient, especially when the Bible doesn't avoid any of them). So there was gas and stuff. By the way, this was billions and billions of years ago (maybe kazillions...who knows). Well, like some kind of cosmic cookie mix, this gas and stuff sort of drifted together. How or why we don't know.

Then, suddenly, it all got so close together that it exploded! KABOOM!

We're talking some kind of serious explosion here. It's called the "big bang" but it should really be called "the really, really, really big bang" because out of this bang came all sorts of gigantic stuff. All of the sudden there were planets, stars, meteors, black holes, and galaxies. As if that's not amazing enough, out of all of this galactic gumbo came an amazing little planet that somebody named "earth." This planet became the perfect place for the spontaneous formation of some pretty important things—like water and oxygen. How or why, there's no way of knowing. Due to the presence of these important, life-sustaining elements, life decided to spontaneously start! WOW! That's like saying that your deodorant decided to spontaneously apply itself or your pop tart spontaneously toasted itself!

Teaching Tip:

This comical account of evolution would be useful to read in its entirety in class as an essay, and it might open up some discussion opportunities. The point is to show how absurd the theory of evolution really is.

Oops, but I forgot to mention—these were pretty primitive life forms. They were single-celled life forms, which are almost as dumb as telephone poles or bowling balls. So, for billions and billions of years these single-cell life forms just floated around in water. Where the water came from we can't really explain, and why it took so long for them to find each other? That's a mystery too! I guess "billions of years" just sounds so scientific that it makes us stop thinking logically. If I can't comprehend a billion years, how could I ever comprehend how this galactic gumbo eventually gave birth to me? Basically, we're expected to just accept it and move on.

So, one day, after billions of years, these single-cell life forms bumped into each other on the micro-organism superhighway, and what do you know? They "hit it off!" They liked each other so much that they decided to stick together, and then they starting splitting into pieces and making more single-cell life forms. These things were worse than rabbits. Before they could celebrate another 10 billion birthdays, there were millions of them floating around in this giant terrestrial soup bowl. It was a big, beautiful world of single-cell families treading water and singing "We Are the World."

Well, a few million years passed before somebody finally decided to break ranks and do something really "out of the box"—like grow a tail or sprout fins. Suddenly, like the fall of some great regime, single-cell life was "out!" Nobody was happy being a single-cell-life-form anymore. Evolving was the "in" thing to do. If you weren't blinking, breathing, swimming, or slurping before too long, you were *nobody*! The world of microbiology was suddenly mass chaos! No fear. No rules. No order. The motto of the day was "just mutate!" If you didn't grow a limb or sprout an appendage, you were nothing more than a "building block" of life!

Eventually the rage settled down as life hit another barrier of development. Everything was "oceanic." Water was it! Life was pretty simple, really. Wake up, swim, eat something smaller than you, swim some more, hope something bigger than you doesn't come along, sleep, do it all again. Day after day, year after year this went on. It only took a few million years for this to get old, until somebody else started thinking "out of the water!" This was the Chuck Yeager of the evolutionary process...the first one to break the land barrier! (And you thought it was the little mermaid.)

One day this thing (no one knows what to call it really) jumped out of the water and landed on the beach like some kind of teenage-mutant-ninja-frog-fish. Don't even try to ask where the beach came from. So now this thing probably went "uh-oh…where'd the water go?" After a few seconds, this brilliant little blob figured out that if he didn't learn to breath air pretty quick, he'd die. (Too bad our peon 21st century fish have lost that evolutionary ability.) Now, after millions of years of development, this thing grew lungs in record time! (It's amazing what we can do when we really have to!) After a quick look around, he figured he liked land, but getting around on fins was pretty hard. So, in another "flash" of evolutionary brilliance he sprouted a couple of legs and arms and became our great, great, great, great, great (to the 15th power) grandfather…the father of the frog family.

Another few million years passed as this frog thing gradually and radically reinvented himself to father every life form known on planet earth. He and his descendants invented the most amazing developmental cycle ever conceived. They developed hair, feathers, wings, heads, beaks, teeth, brains, tails, and trunks. Together they formed the circle of life, but even with all this brilliance they lacked one key ability—the ability to reason. But, they had no idea. They were all content just eating and being eaten. Life had hit another developmental wall. Every day was the same again. Wake up, eat something smaller than you, stay away from things bigger than you, walk around (or crawl), sleep, and do it all over again tomorrow.

The monkeys…they messed everything up this time. They weren't content just being stupid. No…they had to go and evolve again. The process started with walking…on two legs not four. Of course, this took several thousand years of practice, but wow! was the jungle community alive with wonder! Then they started making new noises, losing hair, cooking food, drawing pictures, and thinking logically. This all happened so fast that it took the other species by surprise. One day there was a tail, the next day, no tail. Other species stopped trying to "keep up with the Jones'." It just wasn't worth it anymore. So, before long these monkeys became the dominant species on the planet, renamed themselves "man," and started organizing a civilization. They built mud huts, grew plants, made families, invented things, and started calling the other animals "pets." Except for T-Rex. They called him "sir." Boy, were they glad when "Mother Nature" called in the ice age on him.

Fast forward a few hundred thousand years and you'll find these monkeys writing books, building skyscrapers, driving cars, and even teaching little monkey children how they all got here. They walk, they talk, they think…they have no maker but themselves, no eternity but the grave, no purpose but their own desires, and no authority except "Mother Nature." They are the supreme beings having brutally and tenaciously carved out their own existence from single-celled swimmers to Wall Street stockbrokers in just a few hundred billion years. They've conquered every form of extinction except death and figured out every imaginable question except "why?" Now playing at a theatre near you "The Amazing Multifaceted, Mutant, Monkey-People!"

C'mon! Don't tell me you bought that, even for a second. Anyone who buys into that couldn't have come from monkeys! Monkeys are much smarter than that.

I know…I've over simplified it, but the same tale that's told in modern-day biology books is no less ridiculous. By the way, lest you think otherwise, this stuff is not science; it's religion. There's nothing scientific about it. Chew on these details for a while:

1. Not one shred of valid evidence exists that evolution ever happened.
2. No evidence exists that evolution continues.

3. A universe is no more likely to spontaneously form than a car.
4. No evidence has ever suggested that animals can cross species and produce fertile offspring.
5. Evolution is not observable, which means it's not science; it's speculation.
6. History, true science, and archeology all support the biblical account of creation.
7. Evolution is a religious system of blind faith; the Bible offers a personal relationship of intelligent faith.

II. The way it really happened and why it matters

I guess evolution and creation do agree about one thing. There was a really, really, really big bang. But when and how? The moment that God said, "Let there be..." the universe came into existence in a moment of creative speech. It all happened instantly, and all it took was a few words from the mouth of God! That's how awesome and powerful your God is! He didn't even have to wave His hand or stomp His feet. Just His words did it all.

If you believe that we were put here by the collective efforts of a gaseous explosion, a single-celled revolution, and the circle of life...go directly to the nearest emergency room; your brain may have stopped functioning. The universe itself shows the intelligent, creative design of Almighty God. You cannot see the wing of a butterfly or the pattern in a snowflake without seeing intelligent design. You cannot study the human nervous system or the growth of a newborn baby without seeing that it all shows the touch of a brilliant Master Designer. It takes willful ignorance to believe evolution. All it takes is common sense and simple faith to see creation and to see that *"the heavens declare the glory of God; and the firmament sheweth his handywork"* (Psalm 19:1).

What does all this have to do with you and the decisions that you're going to make? Everything! Your view of these things forms the foundation to the way you think. Your decisions will be made through your value system…or through "what you value." Your value system is founded upon what you believe about life's origin and purpose.

If you believe evolution, then life is nothing more than an accident. You are nothing more than a cosmic freak of nature. If evolution is true, then you have no divine origin, no Heavenly Father who loves and cares about you, no definitive purpose for being, and no absolute truth to follow. You can be your own god. If you don't like something or someone, you can destroy it. If you want something, you can take it. "Anything goes" in the value system of evolution… survival of the fittest. There is no wrong and right, just whatever gets you ahead on the developmental curve. If evolution is true; there is no plan, no reason, and no hope. If it's true, you have no eternal value. There is no significance to your existence, and you have nothing to look forward to. You are just a building block for the next phase of evolution.

The more that people believe this, the more that anarchy will creep into our society. This thinking leads to a lifestyle with no rules, no restraints, and no happiness. It says, "Do whatever you want, whenever you want, and forget about being responsible for your actions." But, it's a miserable existence because there's nothing happy about being "an accident!"

If you believe that God created all that exists, then you believe that He created you! This changes everything about your value system. If God created you, He must care about you and love you. Since God is eternal and God is good,

He must have had an eternally good purpose for making you. Since God knows everything and can do anything, you must be pretty important to Him. He must have something that only you can do in His eternal plan; otherwise, why would He need you? God does nothing without purpose. He wouldn't "make you" just for the fun of it. We're not God's "pets."

III. The beginning of destiny

Second Timothy 1:9 presents it this way, *"Who hath saved us, and called us with an holy calling, not according to our works, but according to his own purpose and grace, which was given us in Christ Jesus **before the world began**."*

In truth, it goes farther back than the beginning of time. Your destiny started in eternity. Eternity is timeless—not bound by the time/space continuum. It has no minutes, days, or years. Imagine that you are standing in a room with one wall that extends forever in every direction. Forever! There's no end to this wall.

Now imagine that there is a flea or a spec of dust on that wall. For sake of illustration, that tiny spot could represent "time" as you know it, from beginning to end. Yes, time had a definite beginning, and it will have a definite end. Time is far less on the wall of eternity than a flea or a spec would be on the wall of our illustration. God had a reason for creating "time." He has a vital purpose that will be accomplished.

"Blessed be the God and Father of our Lord Jesus Christ, who hath blessed us with all spiritual blessings in heavenly places in Christ: According as he hath chosen us in him before the foundation of the world, that we should be holy and without blame before him in love: Having predestinated us unto the

adoption of children by Jesus Christ to himself, according to the good pleasure of his will, To the praise of the glory of his grace, wherein he hath made us accepted in the beloved. In whom we have redemption through his blood, the forgiveness of sins, according to the riches of his grace; Wherein he hath abounded toward us in all wisdom and prudence; Having made known unto us the mystery of his will, according to his good pleasure which he hath purposed in himself: That in the dispensation of the fullness of time he might gather together in one all things in Christ, both which are in heaven, and which are on earth; even in him: In whom also we have obtained an inheritance, being predestinated according to the purpose of him who worketh all things after the counsel of his own will: That we should be to the praise of his glory, who first trusted in Christ."
—Ephesians 1:3–12

God chose you to be a critical part of His eternal purpose before the foundation of the world. The true extent of our purpose for living will only be fully understood when we get to Heaven…it's that awesome!

Since God can see the end from the beginning, He knew everything about you before He made you…including your faults and your sins! (Even the ones you think no one knows about.) Yet, He still made you. He must love you anyway. Nothing you've ever done surprised Him. He's never regretted you. You're not his experiment or his science project.

You are His masterful design—a brilliant part of an eternal plan for the ages. When God was putting together His plan for time and eternity, He came to your birthday and discovered a vacancy. He knew exactly whom He needed to fill that place in the grand matrix of His plan…and He designed you to fit it perfectly. He carefully shaped your likes and dislikes, your gifts and abilities, your desires and dreams to intertwine perfectly with His eternal objective. You have a function, a reason for being, a divine mission assigned to you in eternity past! You have a role in God's drama, significance in God's eyes, a pursuit in God's cause. You have a destiny designed and given to you by God Himself, and you will only be truly happy and fulfilled when you live out that destiny!

God knows you better than you could ever know yourself! He made you. I don't mean He "cookie-cut" you in a mass production assembly line. I mean, He carefully, meticulously hand-crafted you with 100% of His attention. He can do that without losing control of the rest of the universe, because He's God. In fact, there hasn't been one second since the moment of your birth that you haven't had 100% of His attention focused on you!

IV. Understanding destiny

A. Your destiny is unique to you

No one else can be you or be like you. God made you totally unique to His plan, and you fit your place perfectly. No one else can fill your place or carry out your mission in God's plan. You were made to enjoy it, to succeed at it, to understand it, and to truly be happy doing it.

B. Your destiny is awesome!

God is good. He only invents good things, and He only plans good purposes. God is no threat to your desire for a good life. He created that desire, and He plans to fill it with the good life that He designed.

C. You will only be happy as you fulfill your destiny

It's a law of life that you cannot escape. You might "get by," but it can be a lot better than that. Living your destiny presents an exclusive inner joy and contentment that only God can give. You have to believe that there is a level of joy and satisfaction in life that comes only by fulfilling your God-given purpose. When you are living your destiny, you pillow your head at night with real peace and with a full heart regardless of what the circumstances of life may be throwing at you.

D. Your destiny will give you a true sense of divine security

Have you seen how some people deal with tragedy? They go nuts. But have you seen how someone close to God deals with tragedy? They respond completely different. It's still hard, but there's stability, peace, and an unshakeable resolve that guides the life of someone who is living out their destiny. They know that everything is okay. They watch life as if from the grandstand. Nothing can touch them. Eternity is just around the corner, and everything is fine. They're like the carefree kid on summer vacation in the back seat of the car. "Dad's in the driver's seat, and we'll be there soon enough!" What a great way to live life!

E. Your destiny represents true success

So what if you make a lot of money and drive a nice car? So what if you get promoted, and people think you're great? So what if everything falls into place externally, and you appear to be "on top of the world," if you're not fulfilling any eternal purpose! That's a recipe for despair and emptiness. True success is finding and living the mission that God created you for. True success is knowing that you are seeing the script unfold just the way God wrote it in the grand design of His eternal purpose!

F.   Your destiny can be missed

The concept that God sees the end from the beginning might confuse you. You might ask, "How does this mean that I have a free will?" Yet in God's design, there is no conflict between your free will and His master plan. Somehow, in His brilliance, He will see His eternal purpose to completion while simultaneously allowing you to freely choose whether or not to be a part of it. And don't think it's a "set up." Though He may know what your decisions will be, they are no less your free will. When it comes to your destiny, God gives you the final decision. He gives you the free will of accepting or rejecting it. You can live life His way or your way. It all depends on whom you trust more—God or yourself!

G.   Your destiny is now

This is not something that will happen to you someday. It is not a distant possibility; it is a present reality. God has a purpose for you *today*...not just someday! You can live every day knowing that you are experiencing God's perfect will for your life.

In the lessons ahead we'll talk a lot about your future, but you need to understand that destiny begins right now. In addition to this, you might be reading these pages several years into the "Mistake Zone." Perhaps you've made some bad decisions, and you fear that you've messed everything up. God has a fantastic solution for this that we'll elaborate on more in a later lesson. Suffice it to say that you haven't missed your chance to experience your destiny. You may have made some bad decisions, and there may be some consequences that you live with—but God specializes in second chances. Rest assured there are a lot of wonderful days ahead for you in God's eternal purpose!

H. Destiny arrives from God by faith on a need-to-know basis

If you're like me, you'll want to see the whole trip mapped out from start to finish. "God, what am I going to be?" But God reveals His plan only as you need to know. He will make sure you know exactly what you need to know...*when* you need to know it. He will show you very little up front. Don't get frustrated in not knowing. Rest in knowing this...God knows, and you'll be there soon enough...as you follow Him by faith.

I. Destiny is a deliberate choice

It won't happen by accident! Hebrews 11:6 teaches that God rewards them that *diligently* seek Him. Your destiny in God's will must be pursued and must be selected carefully among all the options that the Devil will try to distract you with. It will not be an easy thing to select your destiny. You will be required to enter into the process very prayerfully and wisely. It will take serious consideration, study, prayer, and counsel. It will take complete and unconditional surrender. It *will* be worth it all.

You are the product of a meticulous Master Planner. You are the intentional design of an Almighty God who values you and cares infinitely for you. You are the apple of His eye, the focus of His attention, and the key to His plan for this generation and for the ages. You are exactly as He created you, and you have a divine purpose. You have an eternal mission, and you will never be happier than when you find it and fulfill it.

"Before I formed thee in the belly I knew thee; and before thou camest forth out of the womb I sanctified thee..."
—Jeremiah 1:5

Discussion Questions

1. What are some of the problems with the theory of evolution?
2. How does what you believe about Creation affect your future?
3. Why did God create you?
4. What is "destiny"?
5. List several reasons a person might choose to believe evolution.
6. List several reasons for why we know Creation is true.
7. Why do you think God would create a destiny specifically for you?
8. Fulfilling your destiny is the only way you will ever be truly happy. Why?

Memory Verse

"Before I formed thee in the belly I knew thee; and before thou camest forth out of the womb I sanctified thee, and I ordained thee a prophet unto the nations."—Jeremiah 1:5

Lesson Notes

_____

_____

_____

_____

_____

_____

_____

_____

_____

_____

_____

_____

_____

_____

_____

_____

_____

_____

_____

_____

_____

_____

_____

Destiny Shmestiny...
I Have Plans, Man!

Understanding How Your Plans Mesh
with God's Eternal Purpose

Text

"I beseech you therefore, brethren, by the mercies of God, that ye present your bodies a living sacrifice, holy, acceptable unto God, which is your reasonable service. And be not conformed to this world: but be ye transformed by the renewing of your mind, that ye may prove what is that good, and acceptable, and perfect, will of God."—Romans 12:1–2

"Delight thyself also in the LORD; and he shall give thee the desires of thine heart."—Psalm 37:4

"He will fulfil the desire of them that fear him: he also will hear their cry, and will save them."—Psalm 145:19

Lesson Aim

The purpose of this lesson is to encourage young people to put their well-laid plans on hold long enough to hear this series and consider its profound relevance to their lives. This lesson brushes against the truth of surrender, which will be covered in depth at a later time during the series.

The point is this—some of your students will be listening to this series but dismissing it as they hear it because they've already made their plans. This lesson will encourage them to set aside those plans long enough to give God a chance to teach them something new.

Teaching Outline

I. The truth about your unique design
- A. God creates all of us with abilities, gifts, and desires.
- B. Often our abilities, gifts, and desires become our pursuit, rather than God. (1 Corinthians 10:14; Revelation 2:4)
- C. Finding God's plan begins with setting aside personal ambition.
- D. God has bigger plans for you than you can possibly imagine.

II. The truth about "our plans"
- A. Only God can confirm if your plans are truly right for your destiny.
- B. If you pursue your plans over God, you will never find your destiny.
- C. Your plans could be wrong.
- D. God could change your plans and dreams if He wants to.
- E. God could give you better dreams.
- F. Even good desires can become idols.
- G. Gifts and abilities should be developed but not pursued in place of God.

III. My will or God's will—what will it be?
- A. Jesus set His will aside to follow God's will.
- B. Even good desires can sidetrack you from God's best desires.
- C. Your will must be let go of so that you can find God's.
- D. Misery is doing exactly what you want but never finding your destiny.

five

Lesson Five
Destiny Shmestiny...
I Have Plans, Man!
Understanding How Your Plans Mesh
with God's Eternal Purpose

I. The truth about your unique design

Here's the picture. You're the child, God is the Father, and you have plans. You may have even announced them to God and everybody else in your life. "I'm going to be a (fill in the blank)." To you these plans are as serious as anything else in your life. They are your dreams. They represent the things you like to do and would hope to do the rest of your life. These plans may be self-centered—make money, be famous, have popularity. Or they may be good pursuits—teach school, be a physical therapist, or help the needy. These may even be ministry pursuits like preaching the Word of God, being a missionary, or being a pastor's wife.

Yet, as of this moment, these dreams are yours. Whether or not they are God's cannot be confirmed yet. The only thing you can conclude with any certainty is that these are your dreams. I'm not saying that they don't have a place, and I'm not saying that they are wrong…so stay with me for a minute. I'm only saying you have no way of knowing for sure at this time whether they fit into God's plan, and you probably don't need to know.

God made you with certain abilities and gifts. He created your personality and your likes and dislikes, and the truth is, they will no doubt play a huge role somewhere in your destiny. The danger is these dreams and desires can easily, quickly, and quietly take the very place of God in your heart. They can become your primary pursuit. They can silently become the hunger of your heart and the thirst of your soul. It's usually not a conscious decision, but rather a gradual progression. You may not even realize that this has happened.

Sometimes we convince ourselves that our ambitions are *good*. You might feel pretty good that you're taking life by the horns and making it happen. Actually, this thinking can be a clever cover up for nothing more than self-centered ambitions. I'm not saying that you should be directionless, I'm just saying that your ambitions must not take God's place of preeminence in your heart.

Have you written the script for God, clearly detailing in your mind exactly the way you think it should happen? Are you expecting that He will read it, sign it, hand it back to

> **Teaching Tip:**
> A great way to begin this lesson is to ask the students, "What are your plans after high school?" Have them answer you one at a time. You may even choose to write some of those potential career paths on the board. The entire lesson will encourage them to put those career paths on hold long enough to confirm that they are God's will. Be sure not to criticize those directions or decisions, just get them on the table so they can be discussed and considered.

you, and bless you for doing something honorable with your future?

I've even seen people take this approach to serving God in ministry. The child of God determines very early what he will do for God and what he will not do for God. (i.e.: "I will be a pastor." or "I will be a youth pastor.") And he is sure that God is impressed with such a spiritual decision-making process. But the reality is often that this person has entered into a very subtle form of idolatry. When God leads elsewhere, this child will not follow because he is bent on his own will above God's and doesn't even realize it.

Idolatry is committed any time a person places anything where only God belongs. It may or may not include bowing down to a statue or hugging a tree. For Christians, it is much more subtle than that. Any time you pursue a desire or dream in the place of pursuing God, you have dethroned God. Any time you determine what you will do "for God," you have replaced God with your own desires. The sad part is many times these are God-given desires—good dreams that are never realized the way they should have been, because God was not the object of the pursuit.

Paul warned the Corinthians about this when he said, "*Wherefore, my dearly beloved, **flee from idolatry**"* (1 Corinthians 10:14). Jesus said it this way in Revelation 2:4, "*Nevertheless I have somewhat against thee, because thou hast left thy **first love**.*"

It is entirely possible that you could never fully experience your dreams and desires simply because you were so intent on pursuing them that you left God in the dust! Sounds strange, but it's true…and it happens all the time. Jesus Christ should be your first love, and you should be willing to leave any personal ambition behind to follow Him and to fulfill your purpose in His plan!

You must understand that God will ultimately fulfill every one of the good desires He has put into your heart, but He probably has a less direct route to getting there than you would hope for. Your script for life would probably make a beeline to your biggest dreams, but God's may take a few detours that will make you ready to fully experience His richest blessings.

II. The truth about "our plans"

So, here's what we can conclude about your dreams…your plans.

A. Only God can confirm if your plans are truly right for your destiny

Remember that His wisdom is infinite, and He sees the end from the beginning. Also, He knows you intricately. Just because you *want* to do something doesn't make it right. You may get what you want only to find out later that you really don't want it. That's a common discovery in the "Mistake Zone." You're wise to approach your personal desires with some measure of hesitance. You're wise to guard yourself from totally giving your heart to your desires. See them as a potentially good thing, but also a potential distraction from the best thing!

B. If you pursue your plans over God, you will never find your destiny

You'll be detoured on the "grandfather of all rabbit trails!" Your Creator designed you to pursue Him, not to pursue ambition. Life gets messed up when this gets out of order.

C. Your plans could be wrong

You must be willing to take a neutral position on your plans. No matter how much you want something, always remind yourself that you've been wrong before, you could be now. This is true no matter how "right" your desires feel.

D. God could change your plans and dreams if He wants to

We'll expound on this later, but what a great concept. God could snap His fingers, and *POOF*...you would want something else! That's how powerful He is. You'd never even know what hit you. You probably know someone who is doing something for God that they said they would *never* do when they were your age. What happened? They challenged God, and He took them up on it. He changed their desires. Now, they love doing what they thought they would hate. Personal plans or desires are flexible with God. He's more concerned with your heart for Him. He's not nervous that you "don't want to do something." That's an easy fix for Him.

E. God could give you better dreams

This is perhaps one of the best reasons for holding your own plans with a loose grip. Think of it this way. Compared to God's, you have a very small imagination. What if you have imagined far less than He has? What if His plan is enormously better than yours? What if you get to Heaven, and you find out that God would have been considerably more generous with you than you were with yourself? Now that would be seriously depressing. That would be like listening to the Super

Bowl on a cheap am radio only to find out later that you had a free VIP pass to sit on your team's bench!

F. Even good desires can become idols

Watch out. Deciding to do something "for God" is vastly different than deciding to do "whatever God leads." The first is idolatry. The second is surrender. Make God your first love. Give Him the throne of your heart. He died to pay for it. He deserves that place. He has nothing but good in mind for your future. He sees the future clearly. It's the only sane and safe position to be in. I'm not saying that you should completely drop all of your desires. I'm just saying that they have to be kept in check. Make your plans subservient to God's will.

G. Gifts and abilities should be developed but not pursued in place of God

Those interests and abilities that God created you with will probably fit perfectly into His plan down the road. You should develop them and learn everything about using them, but you should not selfishly pursue them. For example, if you can sing, you should learn how to sing to your full potential. Develop your gift. But the day you set God aside so you can be a singer or the day you decide for God that you WILL sing for Him, whether He wants you to or not...you've crossed the line into idolatry.

III. My will or God's will…what will it be?

This really boils down to a matter of your will and God's will. The Devil will do everything he can to cause them to clash and to cause you to follow your own will. Jesus said in the garden of Gethsemene, *"Not my will…but thine."* In that moment He was battling the greatest spiritual battle of the ages. Thankfully, He set His own will aside for the perfect will of God. Because of His decision, you can know that you're going to Heaven along with millions of other people through the ages.

The human will can be a deceptive thing, even when we think we have good desires. We must not allow even good desires to sidetrack us from God's best desires. It's possible for a person to want something so intensely that he is blinded by it. We can convince ourselves that something is God's will, and never really give God a chance to prove us right or wrong.

If you truly want to find out if your plan matches up with God's, then let it go. If God brings it back to you in His time, then you'll know it's the right thing, and you will enjoy greater fruit in it. If that plan never returns, you can be sure it wasn't God's will, and you can fully expect Him to replace it with a better plan.

The truest test of your first love is this question: if you found out that none of your personal plans were to be fulfilled in God's perfect will, would you still want to follow God? If your answer is "no" then there are two primary problems. First, you've elevated your own intelligence above God's. (You are your own god!) Second, you've failed to truly understand who God is and what His perfect will is really like.

In a nutshell, your own plans may or may not have a place in your future. Don't let that bum you out. If that's the case, believe me, you won't miss them. Either way, you cannot trust your plans; you must trust God. You cannot pursue your dreams; you must pursue God. You cannot allow your desires to distract you from your destiny. One of the most miserable ways to live life is to get exactly what you want, yet never fulfill your divine purpose!

"He will fulfil the desire of them that fear him: he also will hear their cry, and will save them."—Psalm 145:19

Discussion Questions

1. What is the first step to finding God's plan for your life?
2. List three of the "truths" about your plans that you, personally, need to remember the most.
3. How can good desires become idols?
4. What is a sure way to making yourself miserable in the future?
5. What is the difference between deciding to do something "for God" and doing "whatever God leads"?
6. What are some dangers of following your own plans?
7. Write down one gift or ability that God has given you and describe how it can be abused and how it can be developed.
8. Even Jesus put His will aside for God's will. Describe one event in the Bible when Jesus did this and how it affected His life and the lives of those around Him.

Memory Verse

"He that trusteth in his own heart is a fool: but whoso walketh wisely, he shall be delivered."—Proverbs 28:26

Lesson Notes

_____

_____

_____

_____

_____

_____

_____

_____

_____

_____

_____

_____

_____

_____

_____

_____

_____

_____

_____

_____

_____

_____

_____

_____

It's Time to Get Serious
Tool #1 for Right Decision-Making—A Serious Mind

Text

"When I was a child, I spake as a child, I understood as a child, I thought as a child: but when I became a man, I put away childish things."—1 Corinthians 13:11

"Wherefore gird up the loins of your mind, be sober, and hope to the end for the grace that is to be brought unto you at the revelation of Jesus Christ;"—1 Peter 1:13

"The aged women likewise, that they be in behaviour as becometh holiness, not false accusers, not given to much wine, teachers of good things; That they may teach the young women to be sober, to love their husbands, to love their children, To be discreet, chaste, keepers at home, good, obedient to their own husbands, that the word of God be not blasphemed. Young men likewise exhort to be sober minded. In all things shewing thyself a pattern of good works: in doctrine shewing uncorruptness, gravity, sincerity,"—Titus 2:3–7

"Be sober, be vigilant; because your adversary the devil, as a roaring lion, walketh about, seeking whom he may devour:"—1 Peter 5:8

Lesson Aim

The purpose of this lesson is to emphasize a sober mind and to challenge young people to seriously and deliberately begin pursuing God's will for their futures.

Teaching Outline

I. Being serious does not come naturally. (Titus 2:3–7)
   A. Your authorities are commanded to teach you about being serious.
   B. You are commanded to learn about being serious.
   C. Developing a serious mind will be your choice.

II. Gird up the loins of your mind. (1 Peter 1:13)
   A. What is girding up the loins?
   B. How can you gird up the loins?
   C. Use your sober mind to focus on the future.
   D. Use your sober mind to pursue God.
   E. Use your sober mind to respond quickly to God's leading.

III. Be aware of your enemy. (1 Peter 5:8)
   A. You are the target of a ruthless enemy.
   B. You are the child of a loving Heavenly Father.
   C. You must choose to avoid your enemy and follow your Father. (1 Thessalonians 5:6)

six

Lesson Six
It's Time to Get Serious
Tool #1 for Right Decision-Making—A Serious Mind

Now we're going to get into what you need in your "tool belt" in the years ahead. There are several tools that everyone uses to make decisions. For those decisions to be right, you need the right tools. The first tool we'll talk about is "a serious mind."

I know plenty of young adults who let their destiny slip by while they were busy making plans. They were too busy having a good time. They had their friends, their fun, their things, and they were living for the "here and now!" They did whatever felt good, and they rarely gave the next day, or the next year, or the next decade a second thought.

I know young adults that think adulthood is some magical destination. They are expecting some momentous arrival date when the things of childhood will pass, and suddenly the things of adulthood will come clearly into view. For now they are content with Play Station, sports, Twinkies, and TV. They're having a lot of fun! Mom still does their laundry, Dad still pays the bills, and life is good. The refrigerator is full; there's still money in birthday cards; there will be multiple gifts under the Christmas tree (maybe even a stocking of candy); Easter still has a basket of goodies; and summer is still about "being out of school!"

People like this don't see that adulthood is upon them. It's now! While they are waiting for some tribal ceremony where they will shake off the trappings of childhood and accept the mantle of adulthood, life has already started to pass them by. To this kind of person life is still about "playing!"

Paul said in 1 Corinthians 13:11, *"When I was a child, I spake as a child, I understood as a child, I thought as a child: but when I became a man, I put away childish things."*

Being a kid was great! I know there are plenty of kids today with serious trials and loss, but generally speaking a kid's life is carefree. Most American kids wake up with two things on their mind…candy and playing! It's like some kind of obsessive mission that they are on from the moment they wake up to the moment they fall asleep at night. "I must find candy! I must play!"

Do you remember being a kid? During the school day you couldn't wait for recess. You couldn't wait to get home and play. And you knew that God was smiling down on you if you were fortunate enough to get *two* recesses in the same school day! Playing was the theme of life. No matter where you were or what time it was, you were always interested in playing. You could play in church, in the grocery store, and even in the backseat of the car…and you have the scars to prove it!

Yes, childhood was wonderful. Though parts of it can live on forever, you also have to come to terms with the fact that it's time to shoulder additional responsibilities. The fun doesn't completely go away; it just has to share equal time with serious decisions and duties.

I. Being serious does not come naturally

The Bible says in Titus 2:3–7, *"The aged women likewise, that they be in behaviour as becometh holiness, not false accusers, not given to much wine, teachers of good things; That they may teach the young women to be sober, to love their husbands, to love their children, To be discreet, chaste, keepers at home, good, obedient to their own husbands, that the word of God be not blasphemed. Young men likewise exhort to be sober minded. In all things shewing thyself a pattern of good works: in doctrine shewing uncorruptness, gravity, sincerity."*

These verses say that young men and women must be taught to be "sober." The word *sober* literally means "to be brought to your senses and challenged to be disciplined and serious about life." The implication is that someone needs to grab you by the shoulders and tell you how serious life has suddenly become! Apparently being sober doesn't come naturally for young adults, or God would not have placed that command in the Bible.

II. Gird up the loins of your mind

It says in 1 Peter 1:13, *"Wherefore gird up the loins of your mind, be sober, and hope to the end for the grace that is to be brought unto you at the revelation of Jesus Christ;"*

"Gird up the loins of your mind" is a reference to what a runner would do prior to starting his trek. In Bible times, before a man could run, he would have to fold up the long clothing that he wore so that his legs could move with speed and agility. If he tried to run without "girding up his loins" he would be severely hindered and would probably stumble and fall.

Teaching Tip:
This is an easy illustration to use physically in class with the help of a student. Simply get a bathrobe or a long piece of clothing, and have one of your high school young men wear it on top of his church clothes. Have him try to run or walk quickly. This will not only be comical, it will wake the class up and graphically illustrate the point.

In this verse God is commanding you to *"gird up the loins of your mind."* The command is that you would get serious. Take that part of your mind that still wants to spend life playing and eating candy and "gird it up"—wrap it up tightly in control so that you don't stumble and fall. Bring it into discipline so that you can run speedily and respond quickly to God's leading in your life.

A sober mind knows when to be serious and when to have fun. A sober mind understands the stakes and focuses itself on issues that are really important. You could choose to start being serious, or you could wait for your bad decisions to "smack" you into being serious. It's your choice.

"Girding up the loins of your mind" means you must be able to focus your mind, develop it, think seriously with it, and use it effectively. It also means you must guard it from the trash and philosophies of the world.

Let me ask you another question. Do you know what you believe and why? Most young adults cannot give an intelligent answer for why the Bible is trustworthy, why Jesus Christ is God, or why evolution couldn't have happened. If you *"gird up the loins of your mind,"* you'll be compelled to discover these answers for yourself. If you are the type of person that just accepts what you're told, your faith and your future will be unstable because it rests on men rather than on truth.

God has given you a mind, and He has provided a fact-based faith, an intelligent faith. The Christian faith makes sense! It's supported by evidence. Do you know what that evidence is? If not, then find out. Then, when your faith comes into question, it won't crumble. It will stand the tests of ridicule or criticism because you have "girded up the loins of your mind."

III. Be aware of your enemy

"Be sober, be vigilant; because your adversary the devil, as a roaring lion, walketh about, seeking whom he may devour:"
—1 Peter 5:8

This time God brings life to another level of seriousness. He says that you are the target of an assassin. He says that you have an enemy, the Devil, who wants to absolutely destroy and devour you. Stop for a minute and make sure you're comprehending this!

You are a target! Someone is out to get you. Life is not a sandbox. You won't always have Mom and Dad looking out for you. Up to this point everybody else has been sober for you. Now it's time to be sober for yourself! You have an enemy that people have tried to shield and protect you from all your life. As you launch out on your own, you're going to get eaten if you don't start watching your back. It's time to get sober! If you head into adulthood with nothing more than bubble gum, baseball cards, your walkman, and your basketball…you'll be knocked down pretty quickly.

On the one hand, you have a good and loving Heavenly Father who wants to bless and care for you. On the other, you have the father of lies, a roaring lion, waiting to devour and devastate you. In the middle, you have a decision to make. It's the first decision I'm going to challenge you to make right now.

Determine that there will be many moments in the coming days when you will seriously seek God, study His Word, and contemplate His direction for your future. That sounds basic, but many young adults head down the wrong path at just this point. They never realize how serious it all is.

I challenge you to focus your heart, discipline your mind, and set your affection on the things of God. Ask God to help you understand what's at stake and what the risks are. Ask Him to help you "gird up the loins of your mind" so that you can run freely and effectively for Him. Ask Him to mature you and make you ready for the responsibilities He will give you. Ask Him to help you be SOBER.

"Therefore let us not sleep, as do others; but let us watch and be sober."—1 Thessalonians 5:6

My friend, you live in a world of sleeping people. No doubt you have friends that are asleep spiritually. People don't see the spiritual battle for their souls, and they enter into decisions with little advance thought. They make decisions out of sheer whim! They are completely apathetic about the spiritual implications of their actions. It's one thing to buy a new car on a whim (though I wouldn't suggest it). It's another thing to get married, lose your purity, change churches, or have children on a whim. But people do these things all the time!

I dare you to be different. Purpose in your heart to be vigilant and alert. Ask God to bring you to your spiritual senses. Ask Him to mature you. Maturity is not a destination or a tribal ceremony. Maturity is the acceptance of responsibility. Every young adult wants to be thought of as mature, but few choose to seriously shoulder the weighty responsibilities of adulthood. Some are scared. Some are ignorant or simple minded. Some are rebellious. Some are courageous. Which one are you?

I hate to be the one to break it to you, but you're not on your childhood summer vacation anymore. Life is now much more than candy and summer break, and people will quickly bestow the title of "mature" upon you if you will accept responsibility. Life will happen whether you want it to or not. It's happening even now. Are you making other plans? Are you too busy having fun to stop and be serious?

The road ahead will be an odd mixture of growth experiences. It will include plenty of the great things you experienced in your childhood—vacation, toys, the Jetsons, and "Fun Dips." It will also include some heavy responsibility. You'll need the ability to be vigilant and sober.

Soon enough, you'll not only be sober for yourself. You'll need to be sober for your kids…who will spend all of their time obsessing over playing and eating candy. For their sake, learn it now. They need you to be vigilant for them! Their future depends on it.

"But while men slept, his enemy came…"—Matthew 13:25a

Discussion Questions

1. What is "tool #1" for making right decisions?
2. What does it mean to be sober minded?
3. Why is it important that you "gird up the loins of your mind"?
4. To avoid your enemy, what must you do?
5. What lessons have you learned recently that have taught you the importance of being serious?
6. List several examples of how to "gird up the loins of your mind."
7. What can happen to a person who never learns to be serious?
8. Maturity is the acceptance of responsibility. What are some things you can do this week to help you grow in maturity?

Memory Verse

"Therefore let us not sleep, as do others; but let us watch and be sober."—1 Thessalonians 5:6

Lesson Notes

_____

_____

_____

_____

_____

_____

_____

_____

_____

_____

_____

_____

_____

_____

_____

_____

_____

_____

_____

_____

_____

_____

_____

_____

_____

Lesson Notes

_____

_____

_____

_____

_____

_____

_____

_____

_____

_____

_____

_____

_____

_____

_____

_____

_____

_____

_____

_____

_____

_____

_____

_____

If You Are Among the Very "Pure" in Heart

Tool #2 for Right Decision-Making—a Pure Heart

Text

"Blessed are the pure in heart: for they shall see God."
—Matthew 5:8

"Keep thy heart with all diligence; for out of it are the issues of life."—Proverbs 4:23

Lesson Aim

The purpose of this lesson is to help young people understand the role that their heart plays in the decision-making process and to emphasize the priority of keeping the heart pure so that right decisions can be clearly seen. This lesson can be easily divided into two parts—the definition of a pure heart and the maintaining of a pure heart.

Teaching Outline

I. What is a pure heart? (Proverbs 4:23)
   A. Your heart feels life's emotions (feeler).
   B. Your heart discerns life's desires (wanter).
   C. Your heart decides life's directions (chooser).
   D. Your heart includes your intellect (thinker).

II. Your heart is what God sees and cares about.
    (1 Samuel 16:7)
   A. Man sees the outward appearance.
       (Proverbs 22:1; Matthew 5:16)

B. God sees the inward heart. (Matthew 15:8)

C. God cares about both the outward and the inward.

D. God desires inward transformation to produce outward conformity to Christ. (Romans 12:1–2)

III. Your heart can guide you away from God's will. (Genesis 6:5; Deuteronomy 2:30; Numbers 32:7; 1 Chronicles 12:33; Nehemiah 2:2; Psalm 101:4–5; Proverbs 12:8, 20; Jeremiah 17:9; Proverbs 22:15; Proverbs 28:26)

A. Your heart can be destructive.

B. Impure hearts make wrong decisions.

C. Your heart is the lens through which you will make decisions.

IV. Your heart can guide you into God's will. (Matthew 5:8; Exodus 35:5, 21, 35; Job 9:4; Deuteronomy 28:47; Deuteronomy 29:4; Joshua 24:23; 1 Samuel 2:1; 1 Samuel 10:9; 1 Kings 8:61; 2 Kings 22:19; 1 Chronicles 22:19; 2 Chronicles 12:14; Psalm 51:10; Psalm 112:8; Psalm 119:10; Psalm 139:23; Proverbs 4:23)

A. Your heart can be spiritual.

B. Pure hearts see clearly.

C. Pure hearts see spiritual danger.

D. Pure hearts make right decisions.

V. Your heart must be regularly purified.

A. A sinful world creates a dirty heart.

B. Willful sin creates a dirty heart.

C. A dirty heart cannot make right decisions.

D. A pure heart must be purified daily. (1 John 1:9)

VI. How to have a pure heart. (Psalm 119:9; Psalm 51:1–4)

A. A pure heart acknowledges sin.

B.   A pure heart confesses sin.

C.   A pure heart accepts God's forgiveness.

D.   A pure heart changes life's perspective.

E.   A pure heart can be claimed right now.

VII.   Your heart can be changed.

A.   A pure heart is like soft clay in God's hands. (Isaiah 64:8; Jeremiah 18:6)

B.   Thoughts, feelings, and desires can be changed by God. (Ezekiel 36:26)

seven

Lesson Seven
If You Are Among the Very "Pure" in Heart
Tool #2 for Right Decision-Making—a Pure Heart

Your heart is a tool that you will use to make decisions for the rest of your life! You probably never thought of your heart as a tool, but that's exactly what it is.

The fact is there are few things more frustrating than needing a tool for something and not having it. I'm notorious for going to the store and getting something for the house without giving any thought to the tools needed for the job. On top of that, I have the world's worst tool collection. I've spent my fair share of time *beating* on some pipe because I didn't have a pipe wrench. My way of fixing a leaky faucet or toilet is to turn the water valve off and stop using it. I don't get along so well with tools.

I. What is a pure heart?

Your heart is a tool made by God for a specific purpose. It allows you to feel life's emotions, discern life's desires, and decide life's direction. It is a tool of discernment and the source of inner motives. Unless you're dead, this is how your spiritual heart functions.

Literally said, your heart is your mind, your will, and your emotions. Your heart is "what you feel," "what you want," and "what you think." It is the sum total of your innermost being. It represents a part of you that few people see, and it guides and directs you 24 hours a day. It never stops functioning, and you are constantly turning to it for feedback on how to feel, what to think, and what to want.

The Bible says it this way in Proverbs 4:23, *"Keep thy heart with all diligence; for out of it are the issues of life."*

The way you think and feel in your adult life will be determined by your heart. Every time you make a decision, you turn to your heart for advice. It constantly gives you feedback about every experience. Even now, as you read, your heart is the silent commentator in the background, helping you sift through the information, discerning whether it's right or wrong, deciding whether you will accept it or reject it. (Hopefully it's dialed in and concentrating rather than reminding you of your boyfriend or girlfriend right now.) You heart is the seat of your conscience and the unseen influencer in every choice you make.

In order to make right decisions in the days ahead, you must understand your heart and how it functions. You must understand the dangers of your heart and how to keep your heart. If it functions properly it will guide you into God's will; if not, it will guide you away from His will.

II. Your heart is what God sees and cares about

"But the LORD said unto Samuel, Look not on his countenance, or on the height of his stature; because I have refused him: for the LORD seeth not as man seeth; for man looketh on the outward appearance, but the LORD looketh on the heart."
—1 Samuel 16:7

There seems to be two extremes in this particular verse. The first extreme causes me to focus only on my heart and reason that the outward appearance doesn't matter. Quite often this verse is used as an excuse for bad behavior. We reason "Hey, God looks on the heart, so it doesn't matter what I look like, what I wear, or how people perceive me." That's not an accurate application of this verse. The fact that God sees my heart is not a license to live wrong outwardly; it's a reason to make sure that my right living is genuinely from the heart. The Bible teaches clearly that God wants me to care about my outward appearance before men, but not to the neglect of the inward man. If my outward performance doesn't flow from a pure heart of love for God, then it's nothing more than show, which makes me a "man-pleaser" not a "God-pleaser."

The other extreme is that some people focus only on the external appearance and performance as the standard for spiritual growth and nearness to God. If I wear the right clothes, walk the right way, wear my hair right, attend the right functions, and speak the right lingo, people will think I'm spiritual! I can be far from God in my heart but appear outwardly to be very spiritual. The Christian life then becomes a carefully strategized system of outward conformity.

In this way of thinking, I conform so that people will accept me. I play the part outwardly because people believe me, and I never really develop the inward heart of my spiritual relationship with God. This is a very frustrating way to live the Christian life, and it usually doesn't last very long. I will ultimately work harder at covering my bases and keeping up my act than I would at just being genuine with God and others. Plus I'm cheating myself out of a truckload of blessings that come from walking with God personally.

The balance of these two extremes is a commitment to both the heart and the outward fruit of a personal relationship with Christ. You should determine that your outward walk before men will be blameless.

"A good name is rather to be chosen than great riches, and loving favour rather than silver and gold."—Proverbs 22:1

God wants you to "walk worthy of the calling," and He wants the world to see you and your good works and glorify Him because of them (Matthew 5:16). Yet, you should also determine that this life would genuinely flow from an inward walk with Christ. Don't conform; be transformed from the inside (Romans 12:1–2).

"This people draweth nigh unto me with their mouth, and honoureth me with their lips; but their heart is far from me."—Matthew 15:8

Don't let anyone tell you that God doesn't care *why* you do *what* you do! He certainly does. He cares as much or more about *why* you do things as He does *that* you do them. God looks at your heart first, and He knows exactly where you are spiritually even at this moment. He knows what you want, what you feel, and what you think, and more than anything else, He wants you to have a heart for Him.

III. Your heart can guide you away from God's will

Teaching Tip: These Bible references are great to hand out in class and have the students stand one at a time and read them. List these words on the board so the students can get an accurate picture of the potential wickedness of the human heart.

Your heart can actually be a negative influence in your life. The Bible is filled with stories and examples of men and women who were led astray by their hearts. Time does not permit us to delve into an exhaustive study of all the various negative conditions that the human heart can experience, but here are a few. The Bible says the heart can be:

- *Evil*—Genesis 6:5
- *Obstinate*—Deuteronomy 2:30
- *Discouraged*—Numbers 32:7
- *Double*—1 Chronicles 12:33
- *Sorrowful*—Nehemiah 2:2
- *Froward*—Psalms 101:4
- *Proud*—Psalms 101:5
- *Perverse*—Proverbs 12:8
- *Deceitful*—Proverbs 12:20; Jeremiah 17:9
- *Wicked*—Jeremiah 17:9
- *Foolish*—Proverbs 22:15
- *Wrongly Trusted*—Proverbs 28:26

Did you see that list? It looks like a character description off of *America's Most Wanted!* Take a look at it again. That's really a pretty scary list. Realize those words are not referring to what *someone else's* heart can be. This is what *your* heart and what *my* heart are capable of! This is not just the *worst* of humanity. This is humanity *in general.*

The sad part is many young adults make decisions from a heart that is corrupted by one of the above. If there's a time you don't want to make a decision of any kind, it's when your heart is proud, deceitful, wicked, or obstinate (or any other one of the above words). Doing so would guarantee you to be wrong.

Think of it this way—your heart is the lens, or the glasses, through which you will look to make decisions. If your heart is any of the above, you'll be looking through a dirty or tainted lens. You won't be able to clearly see reality, and you won't be able to make a right decision. It will look right from your perspective, but your perspective will be skewed by the condition of your heart. You cannot afford to make life-changing decisions through the lens of a deceitful or an obstinate heart!

IV. Your heart can guide you into God's will

"Blessed are the pure in heart: for they shall see God."
—Matthew 5:8

I must have read that verse a thousand times before it sank in. This doesn't just mean that those whose sins are forgiven will see God in Heaven. I believe there is a deeper application that applies to you right now.

As you head into adulthood, more than anything else, you need to be able to see and discern God at work in your life. You need to be able to recognize His hand. In the face of a million options and opportunities, you need to be able to see which one has God's thumbprint on it. You need to see God, and this verse makes it clear that a pure heart is the only lens through which you can do so.

Teaching Tip:
Hand out these verses to students to read out loud and create a second list on the board showing the potential good things that can flow from the heart.

On the flip side of our last list, the Bible gives another list of words that apply to the human heart. Your heart can be:

- *Wise*—Exodus 35:35; Job 9:4
- *Stirred for the Lord*—Exodus 35:21
- *Willing*—Exodus 35:5
- *Glad*—Deuteronomy 28:47
- *Perceptive*—Deuteronomy 29:4
- *Inclined toward God*—Joshua 24:23
- *Rejoicing*—1 Samuel 2:1
- *Changed*—1 Samuel 10:9
- *Perfect with God*—1 Kings 8:61
- *Tender*—2 Kings 22:19
- *Set to Seek God*—1 Chronicles 22:19
- *Prepared to Seek God*—2 Chronicles 12:14
- *Clean*—Psalms 51:10
- *Established*—Psalms 112:8
- *Wholly for God*—Psalms 119:10
- *Searched and Known*—Psalms 139:23
- *Kept with Diligence*—Proverbs 4:23

These are all positive conditions of the heart. When functioning properly, your heart will interact with God, with His Word, and with His Spirit within to lead and direct you into paths of righteousness. My pastor has said many times from the pulpit, "When the heart is pure, the vision is clear!"

When it comes to spiritual danger, God will use a pure heart as an early warning system in your life. Your heart will be able to discern danger, sense a mistake, and respond quickly to God's leading. What a great gift God has given us in this tool of "the heart."

God's Holy Spirit will be your early warning system and will work through your heart to alert you to spiritual danger. God wants to use your heart to help you see things that others won't and understand things that others miss. People with impure hearts move forward into spiritual danger, never seeing it. People with pure hearts see God's warning and see the spiritual danger before it comes. More importantly, people with pure hearts see God's hand at work in every situation and every decision.

Teaching Tip:

To illustrate the need to regularly purify your heart, use a pair of glasses. Simply borrow a pair from a student or consider purchasing a cheap pair. Cover them with mud before class and then illustrate cleaning them. This will make a good visual and a lasting reminder of how an impure heart clouds our spiritual vision.

V. Your heart must be regularly purified

Do you wear eyeglasses or know someone that does? What must you do to eyeglasses on a regular basis? Clean them. Glasses get stuff on them. People sneeze; people eat greasy foods; the world is just a dusty, grimy place…so glasses must be cleaned on a regular basis. When you wear them for a short time they get smudged, dirty, and blurry. If you go for a long time without a cleaning, it can become quite difficult to see the real world through a dirty pair of lenses. When the glasses are dirty, the whole world looks dirty, and nothing looks right.

Even so, your heart is subject to a myriad of influences through the course of life and must regularly be purified and cleansed. Now, truly, if you've trusted Christ as Saviour, your sins were completely cleansed by the blood of His cross. I'm talking about your day-to-day relationship with God. Your clarity of spiritual vision can easily become tainted and cloudy. Your heart can become smudged with the world's philosophies and filthiness. This world truly is a dirty place spiritually, even when you're committed to fighting the filth.

Perhaps you have become involved in some deliberate sin or habit that is continually wreaking havoc on your spiritual condition. Perhaps through music, Internet, video games, magazines, books, movies, friends, or TV you've been literally bathing your heart in the mud of this world.

While your salvation may not come into question by these actions, your spiritual health and vision certainly do. What kind of spiritual vision do you think these sins create? These behaviors do the same thing to your heart that a mud puddle would do to your eyeglasses. They blind you. They coat your heart with impurity so that you can't see God; you don't recognize His call; and you cannot respond quickly and accurately to His prompting.

Please let this sink in. For years you may have wondered why people have been on your case. Your parents won't let you watch certain TV shows. Your youth pastor has tried to warn you about wrong music. Your pastor has preached against hanging out with the wrong crowd and going places you shouldn't go. Why? Because they want you to be miserable, and they want to take all your "fun" away? No! Because they realize how harmful these things are to *you*. They want you to have clear, spiritual vision. They want your decisions to be right from a pure heart with wisdom and discernment. They want you to see the danger for yourself before it's too late!

I urge you to make these things right for your own sake. The media of this world provides much more than entertainment. It provides a lot of spiritual pollution. Taking it all in with no caution and care would be like wrapping your lips around the tale pipe of a FedEx truck and breathing deeply for a couple of hours. You'd be dead, and I know plenty of young adults who have lost all ability to see God; they've lost all sensitivity to spiritual danger...they are like walking dead people spiritually, because their hearts have been caked with the filth of the world.

If you will make right decisions in the days ahead, they will flow from a pure heart. Thanks to the Lord Jesus Christ and His death on the cross, you don't have to pay for your sins; you just need to acknowledge them before God. He is ready and willing to forgive you. First John 1:9 says, *"If we confess our sins, he is faithful and just to forgive us our sins, and to cleanse us from all unrighteousness."*

VI. How to have a pure heart

So how? How can you, right now, have a clean heart? It's possible, and it's not hard. God already did the hard part, and He's ready and waiting for you to come to Him.

"Wherewithal shall a young man cleanse his way? by taking heed thereto according to thy word."—Psalm 119:9

When David sinned before God, he wrote these words in Psalm 51:1–4, *"Have mercy upon me, O God, according to thy lovingkindness: according unto the multitude of thy tender mercies blot out my transgressions. Wash me thoroughly from mine iniquity, and cleanse me from my sin. For I acknowledge my transgressions: and my sin is ever before me. Against thee, thee only, have I sinned, and done this evil in thy sight."*

While sin always has its consequences, you can come right now to God and be cleansed thoroughly from its presence and power in your life. The Devil wants you to run from God when you're out of fellowship with Him. He paints the picture in your mind like God is angry and ready to squash you. The reality is God is waiting like the father of the prodigal, with open arms ready to welcome you back home. He will not only accept you, He will cleanse you and make you new. He will restore you to fellowship, and He will give you a pure heart and clear vision.

This is God's process of cleansing the heart, and it could happen to you right now. If you feel God's tugging as you read these words, I urge you to find a quiet place of prayer, open Psalm 51, and completely open your heart to God's cleansing touch. Confess to Him, ask Him to cleanse you, and return to your reading a changed person. More importantly, you will see your life through the pure lens of God's wisdom. Your whole perspective will change.

If you feel sure that you are right with God this moment, then make it your habit to regularly return to God through prayer and through His Word to keep your heart clean. It will become tainted without you even knowing it. Your vision will be skewed just from your mere existence in this dirty world. We all must maintain that purity of heart if we are truly to see God in our daily lives.

VII. Your heart can be changed

One final thought before we move on. A heart that's right with God is a pliable thing in God's hands. God says it this way:

"But now, O LORD, thou art our father; we are the clay, and thou our potter; and we all are the work of thy hand." —Isaiah 64:8

"O house of Israel, cannot I do with you as this potter? saith the LORD. Behold, as the clay is in the potter's hand, so are ye in mine hand, O house of Israel." —Jeremiah 18:6

"A new heart also will I give you, and a new spirit will I put within you: and I will take away the stony heart out of your flesh, and I will give you an heart of flesh." —Ezekiel 36:26

When your heart is right with your Creator, some amazing things are possible. Since your heart represents your feelings, your desires, and your thoughts, God can change the way you feel, think, and desire something. It's an awesome process!

Think of it this way. God made my taste buds, right? He made them like the taste of Big Macs. But, if He wanted to, He could make them hate Big Macs and like the taste of drywall screws. (Ridiculous, I know, but work with me here...) He could. He could change my craving for Big Macs into a craving for carpet fibers if it served His eternal purpose.

That's how your heart is in His hands. It's soft and moldable. If you want something He doesn't want you to have, He can change your desire. If you like someone your parents don't approve of, He can change those feelings. If you don't want to be a missionary and eat raw fish, He could give you the strong desire to do nothing but missions and eat nothing but raw fish. If the music you like is wrong, He can give you the taste for the right kind! Suddenly your heart is completely flexible to see and follow God's purpose no matter what. Now we're getting somewhere.

Your heart is an amazing gift from God. It's a tool to be used for a vital purpose. If you keep it clean, it will serve you well. You'll see God, and you'll sense His hand at work in every situation.

"Blessed are the pure in heart: for they shall see God."
—Matthew 5:8

Discussion Questions

1. In what four ways does your spiritual heart function in your life?
2. What are the dangers of having an impure heart?
3. List four characteristics of a pure heart.
4. What is God's promise to you if you keep your heart pure?
5. How does a pure heart guide you into God's will?
6. Why is it important that you care for both your outward appearance and your inward heart?
7. If your heart is the lens through which you will make major decisions, what are some simple habits you can start developing right now in order to cleanse your heart every day?
8. What are some thoughts, feelings, or desires that you would like God to change, and what do you need to do in these areas to allow God to begin molding your heart?

Memory Verse

"Wherewithal shall a young man cleanse his way? by taking heed thereto according to thy word."—Psalm 119:9

Lesson Notes

_____

_____

_____

_____

_____

_____

_____

_____

_____

_____

_____

_____

_____

_____

_____

_____

_____

_____

_____

_____

_____

_____

_____

_____

I Don't Want to Grow Up—I'm a Toys R Us Kid!

Tool #3 for Right Decision-Making
—a Courageous Spirit

Text

"Be strong and of a good courage: for unto this people shalt thou divide for an inheritance the land, which I sware unto their fathers to give them."—Joshua 1:6

"Whosoever he be that doth rebel against thy commandment, and will not hearken unto thy words in all that thou commandest him, he shall be put to death: only be strong and of a good courage."—Joshua 1:18

"Finally, my brethren, be strong in the Lord, and in the power of his might."—Ephesians 6:10

Lesson Aim

The purpose of this lesson is to encourage young people to claim God's strength and to courageously press forward into adulthood, in spite of the intimidating odds.

Teaching Outline

I. Choose to move forward in life. (Genesis 2:24)
   A. Most young adults want to grow up.
   B. Most young adults fear growing up.
   C. Many young adults prolong childhood as long as possible.

D. God commands you to move forward in life. (Exodus 14:15)

II. Avoid defaulting into life.
  A. You cannot decide "not to decide."
  B. The choice "not to decide" is a choice "not to pursue God."
  C. Build your life on good decisions, not on indecision.
  D. Realize you cannot avoid the decision-making process.

III. Be strong and of good courage. (Joshua 1:6, 18)
  A. God called Joshua forward.
  B. Fear tempted Joshua to retreat.
  C. Joshua chose God's strength and courage.
  D. You must choose to either retreat in fear or go forward in faith.

IV. There are five enemies of a courageous future. (2 Timothy 1:7)
  A. Apathy (Joshua 1:6)
  B. Fear (Joshua 1:6)
  C. Ignorance (Joshua 1:8)
  D. Rebellion (Joshua 1:8)
  E. Distraction (Joshua 1:9)

eight

Lesson Eight

I Don't Want to Grow Up—I'm a Toys R Us Kid!

Tool #3 for Right Decision-Making
—a Courageous Spirit

The transition from childhood to adulthood brings many changes and many "paradigm shifts!" (This is another way of saying "a total change in your perspective.") In fact, it can be downright "shock therapy" for your perspective sometimes. Some of these transitions are great—like being able to drive— but others of them are about as much fun as a root canal!

This time of life is very much a proving time. It's a time for you to reckon in your own heart who you will be and how your life will unfold. It's also a time to prove yourself to others—how you will handle college with no parents "on your case"—how you will perform on your first real job—etc. This is the time when others make a judgment call about what kind of adult you will be. Most of all, it's a time for you to either "step up to the plate" in courage or "run for the clubhouse" in fear. In the coming years, you will either move forward in life, or you will try to stay where you are. To move forward, you'll need another critical tool in your "decision tool box"—a courageous spirit.

I. Choose to move forward in life

Remember that "Toys R Us" campaign that sang "I don't wanna grow up; I'm a 'Toys R Us' kid…there's a million toys at 'Toys R Us' that I can play with…"? There's a part of most young adults that secretly sings that song for about four years. Hey, your life has been bikes and trains and video games… why would you want to leave that all behind for bills and canes and insurance claims? For many young adults it goes beyond singing the song or secretly wishing that this easy life didn't have to get harder. They actually try to preserve their childhood. They do everything they can to "not leave home." They stay local. They work local. Local is comfortable. If staying local is God's plan, go for it, but for many it's simply "escapism." They just don't want to grow up.

So, they become twenty-two, twenty-four, twenty-eight-year-old kids. They still live at home, still have their model airplanes and Hardy Boys books, and still let Mom do their laundry. They over-stay their welcome in the land of childhood. Some people do this well into marriage by spending large amounts of time at Mom and Dad's—doing laundry, eating dinner, watching TV—rather than building their own family life. This is not only terrible for a young marriage, it's unnatural in the course of human existence. God commands us to "leave" father and mother…and "cleave" to each other (Genesis 2:24).

In Exodus 14:15, God commands Moses to speak to the children of Israel and to tell them to "go forward." They had finally left Egypt and were standing at the Red Sea. Breathing down their backs was the entire Egyptian army. Impassible water on one side, sure death on the other—but God commanded movement in the direction of the water. Here we have the first amphibious nation! I think if I was Moses I would have asked God if He was thinking clearly. Forward? You've got to be kidding! What? Are we gonna swim this thing?

You know the story. Moses had a choice. Go forward and trust God, or stay put and die. Apparently there was nothing worse than "staying put," so he did just as God commanded him. In response to his faith, God opened the entire Red Sea for the Israelites to pass through on dry ground and then drowned the Egyptian army in the same process. What a great God! What a great story! Uh-oh…there's a practical application.

II. Avoid defaulting into life

Here you are with the choice of "staying put" or moving forward in life. The child in you wants security—wants to stay in your comfort zone. The adult in you is calling for forward motion. God is calling for forward motion. If you stay put, you'll not only be disobeying God, but you'll bring a slow and painful death to childhood as you know it. If you go forward, there are blessings to be had, victories to be won, life to be experienced, and even some childhood to be preserved. You now have to make a choice. Are you willing to say goodbye to the security of childhood in order to become the adult that God wants you to be? It's a tough, emotional, and trying decision, but one that must be made.

I've seen some young adults deal with this time of life by deciding *not* to decide. Somewhere along the line, they just blew a fuse trying to comprehend it all, and they decided not to face the future. The present and the past were comfortable, so they decided to stay there. They chose to avoid the major issues of life.

This kind of person usually gets a decent starter job locally—something slightly better than flipping burgers—and then they just vegetate! Day by day, they just let life happen to them. They exist while the world moves forward around them. They never think about their destiny, their eternal purpose, or their mission in life. They have no motivation, no vision, no desire, and no passion for life. Their goal is to maintain the status quo of their comfort zone. Can I give you some good advice? *Don't do this.*

If you earnestly seek and follow God's will, and He leads you to work locally, stay in your home church, and start your life right where you are, then obey Him. I'm not talking about you. You have no reason to feel insecure about staying close to home if God leads you that way.

I'm referring to someone who doesn't seek God, doesn't pray, doesn't have any desire to become anything; someone who just defaults in life doing and being whatever they can to get by. This is a lazy approach to life that takes advantage of parents and others. This kind of person builds his life upon *in*decision not *good* decisions.

You cannot avoid the decision-making process, even though a part of all of us would really like to. In trying to do so, you will make bad decisions; it's inevitable. It's a natural law of life that you cannot escape. Trying to avoid facing your decisions would be like trying to escape gravity or trying to keep the sun from rising. You just can't do it.

Be like Moses; speak to your heart and tell it to go forward! Determine with yourself that you will move ahead no matter how painful or uncomfortable the transition. Don't be a "Toys R Us" kid the rest of your life. For the present, this will put you on a little tougher road, but there will come a day in the near future when you will truly be glad you made this decision.

III. Be strong and of good courage

Though few transitions are as difficult as leaving home, there are many others between childhood and adulthood. In some ways each transition is a little bit like getting a bucket of cold water thrown on you in the shower. I'm in my thirties now, and I'm still having these experiences from time to time.

For instance: What does "summer" mean to you? When I was a kid, summer meant freedom. From morning to evening we played—no school, no homework, no teachers, no books—just blue skies, bike jumps, and bubble gum! It was awesome. To some extent, you probably still have that perspective of "summer." Well, enjoy it; it's quickly coming to an end. In a short time summer will mean nothing more than regular workdays for you, only hotter.

That's the stuff of adult life. That's the "cold water" of transition. The good news is soon you'll have kids who will play all summer long...on your dime! Isn't that cool...you spent eighteen years playing on your parent's dime...and now it's payback time.

In Joshua 1, the children of Israel are once again standing in front of an impassible body of water. After forty years of wandering in the wilderness, they were almost ready to cross over the Jordan River into the Promised Land. They had one major problem other than the river. Their leader had just died. Moses was gone, and God was planning to put Joshua in his place. It was a critical point for the entire nation, but especially for Joshua. Destiny was knocking on Joshua's door! God himself was telling Joshua that he was the next in line, and from reading the chapter, you get the idea that he was a little bit afraid of the responsibility.

God was calling Joshua to a huge leadership role, which also represented a major shift in his life. He was going from the "comfort zone" to the "pressure zone!" He was being told to lead millions of people into a land of unknown battles. He would be responsible for major decisions with unforeseen outcomes. He was one nervous dude. I'm sure there was a part of him that wanted to run into the wilderness and spend the rest of his life tending sheep. (I think there's a part of that in every leader.) The risks were great; the questions were many; and Joshua had a decision to make for the future of an entire nation.

God's command to Joshua is found first in Joshua 1:6, *"Be strong and of a good courage...."* This same command appears four times in this chapter! It's the very last thing told to Joshua in verse 18, *"...only be strong and of a good courage."* Why would God go to such lengths to emphasize this? Apparently the temptation was to "be weak and fearful." In the light of such huge responsibilities, Joshua would have felt small, incapable, and intimidated. His fear could have paralyzed him from doing God's will, and thus the fate of a nation would be decided.

Joshua chose to rely on God's promises and to shoulder the heavy responsibilities. He chose to believe that God would be with him. He chose to be courageous in the face of intimidation! He chose to face his fear in God's power. Because he left his comfort zone and stepped up to the

Jordan River, the Promised Land was claimed, and the story of a nation was written.

You face the same decision that Joshua faced. There you stand—at your own Jordan River. On one side you have the familiarity of childhood; on the other, the uncharted territory of adulthood. God is calling you to be strong and very courageous. He is promising that He will be with you and that He will give you "good success" if you follow His Word. The task will seem too big for you. The calling will require personal sacrifice and uncomfortable transitions. Your greatest temptation will be to shrink away in fear—fear of the unknown, fear of responsibility, fear of failure. Your decision will impact generations.

I challenge you now to step up to that Jordan River by faith and "go for it!" Choose to have a courageous spirit by God's grace. Know that whatever He asks of you and wherever He leads you, He will be with you. He promises to strengthen you, to guide you, to give you rest, and to bless you. Though you don't see the future, He does! In His strength, you have nothing to fear.

God gave Joshua five statements that reveal five enemies of godly success. These are the things that will keep you from discovering your destiny, and they all revolve around God's command to be "strong and of a good courage."

IV. There are five enemies of a courageous future

A. Apathy

The word *strong* implies that you should be "up to the task" and ready to move on it. It's like someone just kicked you and said, "Get a move on!" Don't be content *not caring* about your future. Get on with it…

B. Fear

There will be plenty of things to be afraid of. Don't be. If God leads you, go forward and refuse to fear.

C. Ignorance

God says you need to know His Word. If you don't know it, you can't follow it, and you'll be spiritually ignorant in life—one of the very worst ways to live.

D. Rebellion

Refusing to obey God's Word puts you in a very dangerous category. Saul rebelled, and God said that his rebellion was *"as the sin of witchcraft"* (1 Samuel 15:23). Rebellion does the same thing to the spiritual mind that drugs and alcohol do to the physical mind. Rebellion causes a person to lose all perspective of reality and do things that just don't make sense.

E. Distraction

This word implies that Joshua could have been distracted from God's will. Determine that you will not be "broken-down" or "torn away" from following God courageously. You will certainly have opportunities to do things outside of God's will, and you must be determined not to be moved.

Bottom line…it takes courage. It took courage for me to hug my family, say good-bye to life as I knew it, and board an airplane to the future. It will take courage in your life to face the transitions that God will lead you through. It will require a conscious decision to step up to the banks of your

Jordan River with a "no fear" attitude to seize God's blessings for your future.

Here is what God says to you in 2 Timothy 1:7, *"For God hath not given us the spirit of fear; but of power, and of love, and of a sound mind."* Let that verse sink in and let it change your perspective on the unknowns of the future. Enter the coming decade with a spirit *"of power, and of love, and of a sound mind."* Remind yourself of this verse when a spirit of fear starts to choke out your courage.

The Devil will do anything he can to make you afraid, hesitant, and doubtful of the future. He wants you to shrink away in fear rather than step up in faith. He doesn't want you to cross your "Jordan." Yet, you must. Many people are depending upon you—people whom you haven't met yet, but people whom you will one day love more than yourself!

I echo the words to you... *"Be strong and of a good courage."* Trust your God to be with you and launch into adulthood with courage! He will never fail you.

"Finally, my brethren, be strong in the Lord, and in the power of his might."—Ephesians 6:10

Discussion Questions

1. Why are most young adults afraid of growing up?
2. In deciding "not to decide," you are actually making what decision?
3. What is the only way to move forward in life?
4. What are the five enemies of your future? Give a short description of how each of these can keep you from moving forward and living out God's will for your life.
5. What scares you the most about "growing up"?
6. The transition between childhood and adulthood is very much a proving time. In ten or fifteen years, what would you like to be able to say about this time in your life?
7. Of the five enemies of the future, which one do you struggle with the most? What can you do to overcome this?
8. Write one decision you have made as a result of this lesson, and outline your "plan of attack" to see this decision through.

Memory Verse

"For God hath not given us the spirit of fear; but of power, and of love, and of a sound mind."—2 Timothy 1:7

Lesson Notes

_____

_____

_____

_____

_____

_____

_____

_____

_____

_____

_____

_____

_____

_____

_____

_____

_____

_____

_____

_____

_____

_____

_____

_____

Lesson Notes

_____

_____

_____

_____

_____

_____

_____

_____

_____

_____

_____

_____

_____

_____

_____

_____

_____

_____

_____

_____

_____

_____

_____

_____

_____

_____

Hey, Buddy, You've Got Boardwalk!!
Tool #4 for Right Decision-Making—God's Wisdom

Text

"If any of you lack wisdom, let him ask of God, that giveth to all men liberally, and upbraideth not; and it shall be given him."
—James 1:5

"For my thoughts are not your thoughts, neither are your ways my ways, saith the LORD. For as the heavens are higher than the earth, so are my ways higher than your ways, and my thoughts than your thoughts."—Isaiah 55:8–9

"For this cause we also, since the day we heard it, do not cease to pray for you, and to desire that ye might be filled with the knowledge of his will in all wisdom and spiritual understanding;"—Colossians 1:9

Lesson Aim

The purpose of this lesson is to explain the vital role that wisdom plays in the decision-making process and to commit the students to asking God for wisdom on a daily basis. This lesson is easily broken into two weeks' worth of material, and the importance of the topic could warrant it.

Teaching Outline

    I. The wisdom of God—"what God sees"
        (Isaiah 55:8–9; Romans 11:33)

A. God sees dangers you cannot see.
B. God sees blessings you cannot see.
C. God understands a purpose you
    don't understand.
D. God offers to let you see and understand
    what He sees and understands.

II. The value of wisdom for your future decisions
     (Colossians 1:9; Ecclesiastes 9:16a; Ecclesiastes 7:19;
     Proverbs 4:5, 7)
     A. Fools die because they don't have it.
         (Proverbs 10:21; Proverbs 1:7)
     B. Wisdom is better than any worldly possession.
         (Ecclesiastes 9:18; Proverbs 16:16)
     C. Following godly wisdom brings true success.
         (Proverbs 24:3; Proverbs 19:18)

III. Finding and applying wisdom from God
      (Luke 2:52; Colossians 3:16)
      A. True wisdom comes only from God.
          (James 3:13–17; 1 Corinthians 1:20–24)
      B. Godly wisdom experiences worldly opposition.
          (1 Corinthians 2:14)
      C. Godly wisdom is more valuable than higher
          education. (Proverbs 4:7; 1 Corinthians 8:1;
          Philippians 2:5)
      D. Godly wisdom is gained by asking God.
          (James 1:5)
      E. God blesses those who ask for wisdom.
          (1 Kings 3:5–14)
      F. You'll never feel like you have wisdom.

nine

Lesson Nine
Hey, Buddy, You've Got Boardwalk!!
Tool #4 for Right Decision-Making—God's Wisdom

I. The wisdom of God—"what God sees"

There is yet another tool that you must possess in order
to make right decisions—the wisdom of God. Wisdom is
spiritual understanding, the ability to see and understand
things the way that God sees them. Wisdom causes you to
see through a situation to understand what's really going on.
It looks "beneath the surface" and discerns things that most
people completely miss. Wisdom is the ability to understand
spiritual truth—God's reality—and to respond properly.

When God gives you wisdom, He gives you the
understanding to see through the rock walls of an issue. He
gives you the perception to see the spiritual implications of
a decision. He helps you think through a situation with real
discernment, rather than rush in, oblivious to danger.

Example: if the concept of "your destiny in God's eternal purpose" is easy for you to accept, this is probably because you have gained a measure of spiritual understanding and wisdom from God's Word over the years. If this concept is new, unfamiliar, or strange to you, then you are probably new to a walk with Christ, and you're simply lacking some spiritual understanding that makes it clear. If you understand the danger of doing things your own way, it's because God has given you the wisdom to see things His way.

God says it this way in Isaiah 55:8–9, *"For my thoughts are not your thoughts, neither are your ways my ways, saith the LORD. For as the heavens are higher than the earth, so are my ways higher than your ways, and my thoughts than your thoughts."* He says again in Romans 11:33, *"O the depth of the riches both of the wisdom and knowledge of God! how unsearchable are his judgments, and his ways past finding out!"* God sees things as they truly are, not only as they appear. Those who see things His way always come out ahead spiritually…it's that simple.

God is literally saying in this passage, "The way I see things is different from the way you see things…and I'm right!"

Have you ever been on a high mountaintop where you could see for miles? When it comes to our lives, our view is limited. We can't see around trees or through mountains. We can't see over peaks or above waterfalls. We can only see what's directly around us.

But from God's vantage point, it's a whole different story. When looking at your life, it's as though He's on top of the world. He sees the beginning and the end. He knows every bend in the road, every turn, every detail. He sees it all and wants to guide you with His wisdom. When He gives you wisdom, He gives you the ability to see a part of your life from His vantage point, and no amount of human wisdom could ever compare to His view!

II. The value of wisdom for your future decisions

I've been continually amazed at how great a difference there is between someone with spiritual wisdom and someone without it. These two types of people can look at the exact same situation and come up with two completely different conclusions and response plans. What seems to be common sense to one seems absolutely foreign to the other. This applies to keeping a marriage together, finding a job, managing your finances, raising your children, and a million other decisions you'll face.

There are two types of people on this planet. There are those who see things the way they really are and respond properly, and there are those who see things the way they think they are, and it takes them a lifetime to figure out they were wrong. The first group learns by seeking godly wisdom. The second group learns by making mistakes.

From job to job, toy to toy, relationship to relationship, they run…looking for some kind of temporary fix to their emptiness. They giggle, they play, they "party" the days away looking for their reward…and there's not one shred of eternal rhyme or reason to any of their madness. They seem happy at times, but if you stop them in the middle of their mayhem, you'll discover that they're on a meaningless journey with no purpose.

Then there's a Christian young adult, maybe you, who is preparing to start his adult life with the winning element— the wisdom of God—right there on his tray. It's there for the claiming. It's there to be understood and applied. It holds all the answers for a successful life. It offers true understanding for godly success. Yet this Christian never realizes the treasure he holds or the wealth of wisdom to which he has access, and he starts his life with no thought of what he is neglecting! The greatest unclaimed resource of life has again gone unclaimed, untapped, unsought…and another life is destined to see things "the wrong way!"

Teaching Tip:

Call out these verses, assign them to a student, and have them stand and read them one at a time in class. Take time to really soak up the true value of wisdom during your class lesson.

Here's what the Bible says about the importance of wisdom in your life:

"For this cause we…do not cease to pray for you, and to desire that ye might be filled with the knowledge of his will in all wisdom and spiritual understanding."—Colossians 1:9

"Then said I, Wisdom is better than strength:" —Ecclesiastes 9:16a

"Wisdom is better than weapons of war…" —Ecclesiastes 9:18

"Wisdom strengtheneth the wise more than ten mighty men which are in the city."—Ecclesiastes 7:19

"Through wisdom is an house builded; and by understanding it is established:"—Proverbs 24:3

"He that getteth wisdom loveth his own soul: he that keepeth understanding shall find good."—Proverbs 19:8

"How much better is it to get wisdom than gold! and to get understanding rather to be chosen than silver!"—Proverbs 16:16

"The lips of the righteous feed many: but fools die for want of wisdom."—Proverbs 10:21

"Get wisdom, get understanding: forget it not; neither decline from the words of my mouth."—Proverbs 4:5

"Wisdom is the principal thing; therefore get wisdom: and with all thy getting get understanding."—Proverbs 4:7

"The fear of the LORD is the beginning of knowledge: but fools despise wisdom and instruction."—Proverbs 1:7

III. Finding and applying wisdom from God

In God's Word, He tells you that wisdom is "the principle thing"! He says to "get wisdom" and to "get understanding." He says that "fools die" because they don't have it and that wisdom is better than money or treasure! He says it strengthens and establishes! Words cannot describe the power and the impact that Godly wisdom will have on your life; it will change the way you see and respond to everything. In some ways these thoughts relate closely to the pure heart in chapter seven, but there are some key principles that you must understand about wisdom.

A. True wisdom comes only from God

The Bible speaks of two types of wisdom. In James 3:13–17, God says, *"Who is a wise man and endued with knowledge among you? Let him shew out of a good conversation his works with meekness of wisdom. But if ye have bitter envying and strife in your hearts, glory not, and lie not against the truth. This wisdom descendeth not from above, but is earthly, sensual, devilish. For where envying and strife is, there is confusion and every evil work. But the wisdom that is from above is first pure, then peaceable, gentle, and easy to be entreated, full of mercy and good fruits, without partiality, and without hypocrisy."*

There are two distinct types of wisdom—an earthly, devilish way of seeing things and a heavenly, godly way of seeing things. The two are opposite; they oppose each other. They cannot co-exist in the same mind. They cannot agree. One is absolutely and undeniably true and the other is utterly false. The scary part is you will make your decisions through one of the two!

The Bible is clear that God's way of thinking is the opposite of the world's. In 1 Corinthians 1:20–24, God says it this way, *"Where is the wise? where is the scribe? where is the disputer of this world? hath not God made foolish the wisdom of this world? For after that in the wisdom of God the world by wisdom knew not God, it pleased God by the foolishness of preaching to save them that believe. For the Jews require a sign, and the Greeks seek after wisdom: But we preach Christ crucified, unto the Jews a stumblingblock, and unto the Greeks foolishness; But unto them which are called, both Jews and Greeks, Christ the power of God, and the wisdom of God."*

B. Godly wisdom experiences worldly opposition

If you see things God's way, through the eyes of spiritual understanding, it won't make sense to people who see things the world's way! Be ready for this. Almost every young adult knows friends or family members who have preconceived ideas of success. If you follow God by faith, it won't make sense to these people. In their eyes, you'll be throwing your life away. Stay the course! When all is said and done, you won't give account to these people, and they won't have to live with the consequences of your decisions. Their opinions of you or your direction mean nothing to your eternal destiny. I'm not saying don't listen to godly counsel; we'll get to that later. I am saying be prepared to be ridiculed for your faith and for seeing things that others don't. It won't make sense to those without God's wisdom.

The Bible says it this way in 1 Corinthians 2:14, *"But the natural man receiveth not the things of the Spirit of God: for they are foolishness unto him: neither can he know them, because they are spiritually discerned."*

Earthly wisdom just doesn't think like godly wisdom does. Yet, time always proves that godly wisdom was right and that earthly wisdom was wrong.

C. Godly wisdom is more valuable than higher education

"Wisdom is the principal thing; therefore get wisdom: and with all thy getting get understanding."—Proverbs 4:7

I've talked to dozens of parents and young adults about their futures and one of the most common replacements for godly wisdom is higher education. We live in a world that worships education. Education is power and influence. Education is the answer for all social and political ills. Education is the idol of many modern day adults.

Please understand, I am not minimizing the importance of education. I'm not saying that wisdom replaces education. They actually work *together*, and you need *both*. I believe strongly that you need the best education you can get. Yet, education by itself will leave you lost in life. Granted, you'll be a smart lost person…but you will utterly fail without godly wisdom. First Corinthians 8:1 says, *"…knowledge puffeth up."*

What good is education if you don't know how to use it and apply it? What good is education if you cannot stay married or rear a godly family? The world is full of very smart people who do very dumb things; they know a lot, but they have no true spiritual understanding.

On the other hand, when you combine a well-educated mind with true heavenly wisdom...now you're headed for godly success! It's extremely important that you get everything you can out of your high school and college classes. You will depend on this knowledge for the rest of your life! I echo the thoughts of God's Word to you... *"with all of your getting...get wisdom and understanding."* Yet, don't fall for the line that education alone is enough. You'll be sorely disappointed.

It seems that one of the goals of higher education is "open-mindedness." At secular colleges and universities you'll be taught that the Bible is closed-minded and that you should be more open-minded. Everything that you believe will be brought into question under the guise of being "open-minded." Most people think that the only alternative to being "open-minded" is being "closed-minded." Yet, this isn't true.

The goal of the Christian should not be either! The Christian's goal is to be "Christ-minded!" Philippians 2:5 says, *"Let this mind be in you, which was also in Christ Jesus."* Your heart and mind should be as opened and closed on every issue as is the mind of Jesus Christ. This is the bottom line, and this will take wisdom.

D. Godly wisdom is gained by asking God

How can you get wisdom? Does it take some kind of special course of study or a lifetime search? Does it require that you graduate from a special school or pass some kind of "wisdom test"? No.

God says the way to get wisdom is to simply *ask for it!* He says in James 1:5, *"If any of you lack wisdom, let him ask of God, that giveth to all men liberally, and upbraideth not; and it shall be given him."* God promises you, if you ask for wisdom, He will not only give it to you…He will give it *liberally.* Wow, what a great promise! This is the world's greatest untapped resource—the Christian's most undiscovered treasure! The Creator of the universe, the Source of all wisdom, the Almighty God of Heaven tells you that you can have a liberal supply of heavenly wisdom…*if you ask!* What an *awesome* gift!

Now, what would you do if I told you that the Source of all true wisdom has offered His wisdom freely and liberally to you if you will ask? Yawn? Fold your arms and doze? "Check out" mentally in Sunday school class or church wishing you didn't have to be there? Well, here's your wake up call, Einstein!

You have *huge* decisions just ahead; you have no idea which way to choose; and you need God's wisdom. So start asking. Ask now. Ask tomorrow. Ask the next day. Decide right now that you won't let a day go by without asking for this great treasure of life. Ask continually for wisdom and know that God will answer your prayer!

E. God blesses those who ask for wisdom

God responds to a person who will ask for wisdom, and generally He's pretty kind to them. In 1 Kings 3:7–14, God came to Solomon in a dream asking him what He could give him. Rather than ask for riches or power,

Solomon said it this way… *"And now, O LORD my God, thou hast made thy servant king instead of David my father: and I am but a little child: I know not how to go out or come in. And thy servant is in the midst of thy people which thou hast chosen, a great people, that cannot be numbered nor counted for multitude. Give therefore thy servant an understanding heart to judge thy people, that I may discern between good and bad: for who is able to judge this thy so great a people?"*

Solomon's request made God so happy that He said, *"Because thou hast asked this thing, and hast not asked for thyself long life; neither hast asked riches for thyself, nor hast asked the life of thine enemies; but hast asked for thyself understanding to discern judgment; Behold, I have done according to thy words: lo, I have given thee a wise and an understanding heart; so that there was none like thee before thee, neither after thee shall any arise like unto thee. And I have also given thee that which thou hast not asked, both riches, and honour: so that there shall not be any among the kings like unto thee all thy days. And if thou wilt walk in my ways, to keep my statutes and my commandments, as thy father David did walk, then I will lengthen thy days."*

While young adults your age are busy asking God for cars, spouses, jobs, and things, I urge you to follow Solomon's example. Rather than asking God to fulfill your plans or dreams; rather than asking Him to do what you want; rather than asking Him to reveal His will to you…start asking for wisdom!

Most spiritual young people are consumed with needing to know God's will. Every time they pray, they're begging God to show them what they should do with their lives. While seeking God in this way is commendable, this type of praying often misses the most important prayer. God will reveal His will in His time. He hasn't hidden it for you to hunt down like "lost treasure." This is not some kind of cosmic Easter-egg hunt. He will show you what He wants when He wants. What you need now is the wisdom to see and understand God today!

More than anything else, you should be asking God for wisdom. He will not only answer you fully, but He will also give a lot that you didn't ask for. I challenge you right now to permanently place wisdom at the top of your prayer list for the rest of your life; you'll need it every day!

F. You'll never feel like you have wisdom

The thing that makes it difficult to ask for wisdom is that it is intangible! Hey, if I ask God for a job or a car, and He answers—I can see it; touch it; experience it. I can tell everybody else to look at the answer to my prayer! It's a great experience. Asking for wisdom seems somewhat obscure in comparison; therefore, many people never get around to it. We're so distracted by our selfish prayers that we forget what we really need!

You'll never really feel like you have wisdom. You could spend a lifetime asking for it and never be able to pinpoint a moment when you actually felt "wise." Don't expect to ask God and…*BOOM*…lightning strikes one day, and suddenly you're a "wise guy!" It's not a feeling or an electrifying experience. There's no magic moment, no arrival date, no special package in the mail, and no "paranormal experience." It's rather dry and "feelingless."

You'll only know that God gave you wisdom when you've lived long enough to look back on His guidance in your life.

Here's how it works. Start asking now. Trust by faith that God is giving it to you, even though you don't know it or feel it. Keep on asking. Live twenty years. Turn around and look back. Suddenly you'll see decision after decision that you could have blown, but somehow every one of them was made right. That's wisdom! That's how God will answer your request for wisdom.

Wisdom is not a Christmas present that you can open; it's not a winning game piece you can claim; but it's just as real and far more valuable. The best part— you don't have to be some lucky "one-in-forty-billion" to have it…just ask for it—anytime, anywhere…and *BOOM*…you can have it! (Without the *BOOM!*)

So, what will it be…earthly wisdom? Are you interested in running around for the rest of your life collecting losing game pieces…spending your life on frivolous pursuits that mean nothing? Or will it be heavenly wisdom? …Gained by simply asking. You can live your life seeing things for what they really are— seeing them the way that God sees them.

Follow the pattern of Jesus in Luke 2:52, *"And Jesus increased in wisdom and stature, and in favour with God and man."* Go to God; go to His Word and start asking for wisdom today! The Bible says in Colossians 3:16, *"Let the word of Christ dwell in you richly in all wisdom."*

Don't throw away the most valuable resource available to you. Decide that tool #4—the wisdom of God—is one that you won't miss out on. Start asking right now.

"Wisdom is the principal thing…"—Proverbs 4:7

Discussion Questions

1. What is godly wisdom?
2. What two things does God see in your future that you cannot see?
3. What kind of people succeed and why?
4. How do you gain godly wisdom?
5. Why is it so important that you ask God for wisdom every day?
6. Think about a decision you made in the past that you regret because you didn't ask God for wisdom. Describe this event and how the consequences might have been different if you had God's wisdom on the matter.
7. Godly wisdom is more valuable than higher education. Why?
8. Why should you start daily seeking God's wisdom now, instead of waiting until you have big decisions to make?

Memory Verse

"Wisdom is the principal thing; therefore get wisdom: and with all thy getting get understanding."—Proverbs 4:7

Lesson Notes

_____

_____

_____

_____

_____

_____

_____

_____

_____

_____

_____

_____

_____

_____

_____

_____

_____

_____

_____

_____

_____

_____

LESSON TEN

Believing is Seeing

Tool #5 for Right Decision-Making—A Life of Faith

Text

"Now faith is the substance of things hoped for, the evidence of things not seen. For by it the elders obtained a good report. Through faith we understand that the worlds were framed by the word of God, so that things which are seen were not made of things which do appear. By faith Abel offered unto God a more excellent sacrifice than Cain, by which he obtained witness that he was righteous, God testifying of his gifts: and by it he being dead yet speaketh. By faith Enoch was translated that he should not see death; and was not found, because God had translated him: for before his translation he had this testimony, that he pleased God. But without faith it is impossible to please him: for he that cometh to God must believe that he is, and that he is a rewarder of them that diligently seek him."—Hebrews 11:1–6

Lesson Aim

The purpose of this lesson is to help your students understand the role that faith plays in the Christian life and in the process of making right decisions. The students will be challenged to step out in obedience to God, even when the circumstances don't seem to make sense to human reasoning.

Teaching Outline

I. God relates to us by faith. (Hebrews 11:1–6; Psalm 32:8; Psalm 34:8, 22)
   A. People say, "Show me, and I'll believe."
   B. God says, "Believe me, and I'll show you."
   C. Faith doesn't work by sight. (Genesis 6)
   D. Faith doesn't work by sense.

II. Why did God choose faith? (1 Peter 5:4; James 1:12; 2 Timothy 4:8)
   A. God could have chosen to relate to us by sight.
   B. God purposefully designed to hide Himself and to relate to us by faith.
   C. God gives us intelligent faith, not blind faith.
   D. God proves our faith after it is expressed.
   E. Our faith fulfills God's eternal purpose.

III. What is faith?
   A. Faith is not a force.
   B. Faith is simply trusting God. (Luke 1:38; 1 Corinthians 13:12)
   C. Faith opposes human reasoning. (Exodus 4:21)
   D. Faith requires circumstances that do not make sense.
   E. Faith is always rewarded by God. (Hebrews 11:6)

IV. How does God respond to faith?
   A. Faith greatly pleases and delights God.
   B. Faith moves God into action in our lives.
   C. Faith allows God to do the impossible.
   D. Faith always brings God's best rewards.

ten

Lesson Ten
Believing is Seeing
Tool #5 for Right Decision-Making—A Life of Faith

I. God relates to us by faith

There's yet one more tool to throw into your "belt" before
we wrap up by talking about how to use these tools to make
right decisions. In order to really find your destiny you must
be willing to live by faith.

What is faith? Hebrews 11:1 says, *"Now faith is the
substance of things hoped for, the evidence of things not seen."*
Faith is the substance of the things you hope for—happiness,
true success, purpose in life, God's blessings. If you will
ever discover your true destiny you must realize that its very
substance (its reality) will be found through faith.

Faith is the evidence for things that you cannot see.
Think about that. You cannot see the family God will give
you, the life He will let you live, the dreams He will allow

you to fulfill; yet you know these things exist in God's mind. How? By faith. You believe in your heart that God has written your life's story according to His eternal purpose, and all you have to do is allow Him to reveal it to you. That belief is faith, and that faith is the substance and the evidence of your destiny.

Worldly wisdom doesn't understand this rationale! Most people would say "Show me, and I'll believe." God says, "Believe Me, and I'll show you!" Yet, in the mind of the typical unsaved man, it doesn't make sense that you would completely leave your destiny in the unseen hands of an unseen God. That's much too risky. It feels like a blind approach to life. Yet, that's the only way to truly guarantee yourself to find your destiny.

Whatever your future holds, God wants you to trust Him completely by faith. He wants to lead you into decisions where you must trust Him by faith, not knowing the outcome. He wants to be your full-time guide. If you have your life all figured out, well planned, and mapped in your mind…you're simply not living by faith. God will ask you to surrender your "life-map" and let Him create a new one—one you haven't seen! Sound too risky? Not at all…it just sounds like faith!

The Bible is filled with stories of faith and God's response to faith. Consider Noah in Genesis 6 when God commanded him to build an ark. Noah didn't live near water, had no idea what an ark was, and had never seen rain. Yet, in spite of all of this *sight-based* information, Noah chose the *faith* path. God's request seemed way out of line. His command to Noah was far beyond the bounds of normal reason. No matter how you look at it, it didn't make any sense! Nevertheless, God was right.

Consider that God asked Abraham to sacrifice his only son Isaac. This was the son that God promised to bless—the father of a "great nation," and now God was asking that he be killed! This sounds ridiculous. Though the request was bizarre, Abraham willingly trusted God by faith.

If you were Joshua preparing to fight the city of Jericho, what would you expect from God? You'd probably be looking for miraculous answers to prayer like tanks, machine guns, angel armies, and nuclear arsenals. Instead, God commanded Joshua to march around the city. March around the city? You've got to be kidding! What's that supposed to accomplish? It just didn't make sense, but he obeyed anyway, and God won the victory. I wonder how many armies around the world began "marching around cities" after that, thinking Joshua had discovered some kind of strange "seismic" advantage?

God commanded the leper Naaman to wash seven times in a muddy river to be healed. At first Naaman refused. Finally after some prodding from people who cared about him, Naaman dunked himself seven times in the Jordan River. He must have felt pretty stupid as people passed by. By about the fifth and sixth dunk he must have really been embarrassed that there was no hint of a cure!

Now that seventh dunk—that's the one that did the trick! Suddenly the leprosy was gone—all because of simple faith.

It wasn't the muddy water that healed Naaman. It wasn't marching around the city that made Jericho's walls fall down. God wasn't really interested in having Isaac killed or in teaching Noah how to parasail. He was interested in His faith relationship with each individual. Faith is the central theme of every intervention that God has ever had in human life.

He led Joseph into slavery and prison where Joseph's undying faith finally resulted in blessing and success. David chose to take on Goliath by faith. Peter chose to walk on water by faith. Daniel refused to defile himself with the king's meat—by faith. On and on the stories go. Person by person, you see God bless the faith of those who will trust in Him. God promises in Psalm 34:8, *"O taste and see that the LORD is good: blessed is the man that trusteth in him."* Again in verse 22 He says, *"The LORD redeemeth the soul of his servants: and none of them that trust in him shall be desolate."* The faith life is the most secure and sure way of living life. The way that makes the least sense actually makes the most sense!

II. Why did God choose faith?

Could God have chosen to relate and interact with you by sight? Of course He could have. He does with the angels. He does with those already in Heaven. Why not with you and me? Why doesn't He just pull back the veil and let us see into eternity? Wouldn't it be great to see Heaven from Earth? Wouldn't it be great if, on every kid's fifth birthday, God came to the party? "Hello, Bobby, I'm God! Here's a gift for you! By the way…POOF…I just turned your water into milk to go along with that delicious cake and ice cream I made!"

Everyone would believe in God then. That would make everyone want to be saved. He could do these things if He wanted. So, why did God determine that our relationship with Him is based upon faith?

The answer goes back to His eternal purpose. Outside of the boundary of time, God has an eternal purpose that works all things together for good under the Lordship of Jesus Christ. Ephesians 1:10–12 says it this way, *"That in the dispensation of the fulness of times he might gather together in one all things in Christ, both which are in heaven, and which are on earth; even in him: In whom also we have obtained an inheritance, being predestinated according to the purpose of him who worketh all things after the counsel of his own will: That we should be to the praise of his glory, who first trusted in Christ."*

You are an intricate part of a timeless plan to "gather together in one all things in Christ." In other words, you are a part of God's eternal plan to reconcile all things back to Christ, to undo the effects of the angelic rebellion, and to restore perfect good back into eternity…for all of eternity.

The fact that you believe in God, trust Him fully, and follow Him in faith having never seen or heard Him brings great glory to Him in the courtroom of eternity! In order for your part in God's plan to even matter, your relationship to Him had to be based upon faith. He chose that faith would be the only "line of communication" between our physical world and His eternal existence.

In a sight-based universe, that's very difficult to comprehend, yet it's true. Somehow God's plan for you in eternity is predicated upon the fact that you must "relate" to Him in time and space strictly by faith. The rules of our existence and the purpose of our creation hinge upon relating to God without seeing or hearing Him physically.

Why? I believe that the biggest reasons for our *faith* existence go beyond our comprehension (remember *"my ways are not your ways…"*), but one reason may well be this. Consider how your testimony of choosing to love God by faith, having never seen Him, might weigh in the courtroom of condemnation of a fallen angelic host who rebelled against God "by sight!" Just a thought (1 Corinthians 6:3 says, *"Know ye not that we shall judge angels?"*).

Think of it this way. The Bible is clear that God will "reward" our faith (1 Peter 5:4; James 1:12; 2 Timothy 4:8). When you stand before Him in eternity, at the culmination of His eternal plan, your faith will be a trophy that will glorify God and justify His judgment on sin. Your faith will be an inarguable testimony against Satan and his fallen hosts as sin is judged and cast forever into a lake of fire. Your willingness to trust God without seeing Him or hearing Him will be a witness in the courtroom of the universe to God's justice and goodness, and your faith-life will be recognized and rewarded by God.

Accept the fact and even enjoy the fact that you cannot see or hear God. That's what faith is all about. That's what your existence is all about. Anticipate the thought that in God's economy…believing is seeing!

III. What is faith?

It's easy to believe in and trust in God when everything is going your way. Most Christians have no problem admitting that God is blessing them when they get a raise, a special gift, or a unique blessing. It's natural to believe in God and recognize His goodness when you have a new car, money in your birthday cards, good grades, and nice Christmas gifts.

In fact, there's a false teaching in some circles that faith is almost like a "force." Some people treat God like a genie, and faith is what binds Him to do what you want. If you have enough faith, you can make God do anything or give you anything, as though "your wish is His command!" If you are sick, God will heal you. If you are poor, God will make you wealthy. If you want something…simply have faith and claim it!

By this false theology, faith becomes nothing more than a self-centered tool of manipulation to get exactly what you want from God. In the end, this false brand of faith is very disappointing because you'll never feel like you have enough faith when things don't go your way. Eventually you will stop living for God and trusting Him at all.

No, faith is not a force, and having faith does not mean that everything will go your way. It's when things don't go your way that faith really "kicks in!" Up to that point you're trusting God by sight.

What do you do when God takes someone you love? What happens when you follow God with all of your heart and things don't go well? How do you respond to God when He leads you into a trial, controversy, or sorrow? Living the faith-life means you trust God fully and rely upon His strength regardless of what He chooses to do. Living by faith means you trust God even when your whole world is falling apart. Faith is knowing in your heart that God is working all things together for good when you can see nothing but bad!

Faith is Joseph wrongfully put in jail but never turning his back on God. Faith is Paul and Silas in jail singing praises to God. Faith is Noah being ridiculed for building a gigantic boat in his front yard, but trusting God anyway. Faith is Peter stepping out of the boat in the middle of a storm (The storm that God sent him into!). Faith is three Hebrew young men being thrown into a fiery furnace not knowing what God would do, but trusting Him anyway.

Job had faith, even though God permitted the total destruction of his entire family and estate. Paul had faith, even though he was beaten, imprisoned, shipwrecked, and stoned. On top of that, God refused to take away his thorn in the flesh, but he still trusted Him.

Mary and Joseph had faith to trust God even though it meant their dreams and ideas for happiness would suddenly change. How would you like having to explain to your family that you were expecting a child from God? It didn't make sense that God would ask Mary and Joseph to endure the loss of their good reputations for His eternal plan, but they accepted His plan by faith. Mary herself said to the angel, *"Behold, the handmaid of the Lord. Be it unto me according to thy word"* (Luke 1:38). By the way, just in case it's never occurred to you, her decision at that moment affected you!

Faith is following God when He doesn't make sense, regardless of the outcome. Faith is knowing that this world is temporary and that reality is just one breath away in eternity. Faith understands that now we *"see through a glass darkly, but then face to face"* (1 Corinthians 13:12). Faith is holding the physical world loosely so you can cling to the unseen eternal God!

God came to Moses in Exodus 4:21 and commanded him to tell Pharaoh to release the Hebrews. In the same verse, He told Moses that Pharaoh's heart would harden and he would not listen! Think about that. My question would have been, "So why go?" Why would God send Moses into a situation knowing that it wouldn't work! He deliberately commanded Moses to go on a failing mission. He knew the end from the beginning. He knew that Pharaoh would not listen. It didn't make sense for Moses to accept this command, but he did anyway.

This is a key characteristic of the faith-life. God will probably lead you into a situation that doesn't make sense. He will put you in a predicament where you are inadequate and unable to do His command. He may ask you to do something you just don't want to do. Often He will lead you directly into the face of impossibility!

IV. How does God respond to faith?

Chances are, at first, His will for your life won't make sense by sight. In many ways, it will probably contradict all human reasoning and rationale. You won't be able to see the end from the beginning. When you come to the point that you will follow Him anyway…you will be living by faith! When you arrive at the determination that you will trust Him blindly, knowing *"that He is and that He is a rewarder of them that diligently seek Him"* (Hebrews 11:6), you are living the faith life.

I've discovered that no matter what God asks me to do, He will give me a love for it and the ability to do it! I've also discovered that eventually He aligned my responsibilities more closely to my personal dreams and God-given desires… but not until He was sure I would follow Him when He didn't make sense.

We live in a world where people want guarantees. Before you buy a computer, you'll probably check out the warranty. Before some people get married they make a "prenuptial agreement" to protect themselves "just in case." When you make a major purchase you read the fine print to safeguard that you aren't getting "ripped off." On and on it goes.

With the faith-life, the guarantee doesn't come until after you've signed the "dotted line!" But mark it down; it always comes! God's Word is true, His heart is good, and His promises never fail. He is faithful to those who trust Him. You will never read of a Bible character or meet a person who truly trusted God and was "let down!" It is an impossibility.

It just cannot happen. After you've made the commitment to follow God by faith, He will always sustain you.

This is the process of the Christian life: life doesn't make sense, so you trust God. You step out by faith into the unknown. God responds to your faith and cares for you. You see God at work in your life in a real way. You believe more strongly that God is real and that He is right. Your faith becomes stronger for future steps of faith. The process begins all over again!

It's a wonderful progression of spiritual growth, but most people never take the first faith step to experience it. Most Christians never get very far in discovering the faith-life because they trust what they can see more than they trust God. As a result, their spiritual journey is stifled. So, I challenge you to step boldly into a life of faith. Expect that your future will hold many unknowns. Expect that God will deliberately "not make sense" to you. Expect Him to bring you into impossible situations where your faith can be expressed and enlarged.

Then, when you're standing on the edge of a sight-based life, looking into the "nothingness" called your future...have confidence that when you step forward, God will catch you. Have the boldness to follow what you cannot see, regardless of how stupid some people think you are. Then, when you follow in faith, and God leads you into a situation that has you scratching your head and wondering where God went wrong...trust Him anyway.

Just about the time you're thinking "Uh, Lord...I didn't see this in the fine print of our agreement" just tear up the contract, give God carte blanche with your life; and from that point, it will only be a matter of time before you see Him mightily at work in your life! That's when it really gets exciting.

You're the quarterback, God is the coach, and sometimes He's going to call a play that just doesn't make sense to you! Do yourself a favor. Save yourself the embarrassment, and potentially the ruined life. No matter how strange you think the play sounds. No matter how backwards it seems to your psyche. No matter how mixed up you think it is...don't do the unthinkable. Don't change the call.

Just run the play...God knows exactly what He's doing!

"...I being in the way, the LORD led me..."—Genesis 24:27

Discussion Questions

1. What is the difference between God's view and people's view of faith?
2. Why did God choose faith as a means of relating to us?
3. Based on the information given in this lesson, what is faith?
4. What happens when we exercise faith in our lives?
5. Thinking about your own future, describe how your actions and thinking might be different if you lived by sight and if you lived by faith.
6. Compare and contrast intelligent faith with blind faith.
7. In what area of your life right now do you struggle with the most when it comes to having faith in God? Why should you trust Him in this area?
8. List three examples in the Bible of how God blessed someone because they had faith.

Memory Verse

"O taste and see that the LORD is good: blessed is the man that trusteth in him."—Psalm 34:8

Lesson Notes

_____

_____

_____

_____

_____

_____

_____

_____

_____

_____

_____

_____

_____

_____

_____

_____

_____

_____

_____

_____

_____

_____

_____

_____

_____

Lesson Notes

_____

_____

_____

_____

_____

_____

_____

_____

_____

_____

_____

_____

_____

_____

_____

_____

_____

_____

_____

_____

_____

_____

Only Weird People Wear Their Pants Backwards

Step #1 for Right Decision-Making
—Refuse To Trust Yourself

Text

"Trust in the LORD with all thine heart; and lean not unto thine own understanding. In all thy ways acknowledge him, and he shall direct thy paths."—Proverbs 3:5–6

Lesson Aim

The purpose of this lesson is to challenge your students to place their full 100% trust in God, and to refuse to trust their own understanding or perspective.

Teaching Outline

I. The problem with self-trust
    A. We cannot see what God sees.
    B. We do not know what the future holds.
    C. We are prone to be wrong.
    D. Trusting self directly defies God.

II. Refusing to trust yourself (Proverbs 3:5–6)
    A. People who make right decisions do not trust themselves.
    B. People who make right decisions recognize their own weaknesses.
    C. People who make right decisions choose to trust God fully.

III. The subtle power of self-deception (Romans 7)
   A. It is natural to lean to our own understanding. (Proverbs 3:5)
   B. It is possible to deceive ourselves away from our destiny. (James 1:14)
   C. We must reject emotion and follow God's Word. (Galatians 2:20; 1 John 3:20)
   D. Feelings will always follow obedience to God.

IV. Putting your trust to the test
   A. Write out your future dreams and plans on a blank sheet of paper.
   B. Dream big and be specific.
   C. Get a big red marker and write "DO NOT TRUST THIS" across the top.
   D. Hang it in a prominent place.

eleven

Lesson Eleven
Only Weird People Wear Their Pants Backwards
Step #1 for Right Decision-Making
—Refuse To Trust Yourself

1. The problem with self-trust

Many teenagers and young adults are very much like my three-year-old son, Lance, when he put his own pants on backwards! They are making decisions, taking steps, and moving forward in life—on their own. They are so proud of the fact that they are "grown up" that they've completely missed the fact that they still don't know much. They are doing things like accepting jobs, enlisting in the military, choosing colleges, buying cars, getting credit cards, dating strangers, falling in love, getting married, and having children—but they're doing them all the wrong way. They're doing them with no biblical direction, no prayer, and no godly counsel.

Obviously, *doing* these things isn't wrong, but it is possible to *do* them the wrong way. It's possible to go about these things in all the wrong way, to "put life on" backwards.

The crazy thing is these people are always "right in their own eyes," but their mistakes are glaringly obvious to others around them. The decisions they are making are as obviously backwards as Lance's pants were, but they are firmly convinced that everything's okay! And you usually can't reason with this type of person. You can see as plain as day that they are making a wrong choice, but they are completely oblivious to it. They are blinded by their own ignorance and unwilling to listen to anyone else. In fact, if you try to intervene and lovingly interfere, you might even become the object of anger or resentment.

What's the problem? Two words—trusting self. Lance was trusting in himself to get his pants on properly, and he was wrong. In his limited view of life and his minimal understanding of the clothing industry, he had credited himself with far more knowledge and understanding than he really had. He was self-confident.

Many young adults have this same problem. They are completely self-confident. They fail to see how much they don't know and how vulnerable to mistakes they really are. (By the way, we're all vulnerable, it's just that young adults seem to have a tough time admitting that.)

II. Refusing to trust yourself

So, let me be completely honest with you. As painful as this may be, you'll be way ahead of the game if you'll take this bitter pill and swallow it now. The first step to actually making a right decision is to refuse, *absolutely refuse*, to trust yourself. I know it sounds backwards when the world is screaming at you, "It's your life, do whatever feels good!" But it's the Bible truth.

Remember that the Lord calls us "sheep." When is the last time you heard of a major NFL team or a college team named "the mighty, mighty *Sheep?*" I don't think so. Why? Sheep are known for being the dumbest animals on the planet. They are easy to scare, easy to prey upon, and very easy to mislead. Sheep must be led to safety, led to water, and led to food. They must be carefully watched over and guarded, and the Bible says that we are just like them!

We are weak and helpless, and we cannot guide or protect ourselves. When it comes to the reasons and intricacies of God's eternal purpose, we're just plain dumb. We're easily deceived and misled, and we are utterly dependent upon the Good Shepherd to watch and guide over us.

"Trust in the Lord with all thine heart and lean not unto thine own understanding. In all thy ways acknowledge Him and He shall direct thy paths."—Proverbs 3:5–6

As we've explored the tools of a sober mind, a pure heart, a courageous spirit, a life of faith, and the wisdom of God, they all begin to be applied in this principle. All of these "tools" should lead you to the conclusion that you cannot and will not see things the way that God sees them, and this conclusion leads you to a decision. Whom will you trust? Whom will you rely upon? Whose viewpoint will you adopt as you make decisions in your future?

If anything that you've heard thus far has sunk in, hopefully you are instantly thinking, "God, of course. Who else?"

That's good, but keep listening.

III. The subtle power of self-deception

The implication of Proverbs 3:5–6 is that we all have the tendency to "lean to our own understanding." It's natural for you to just rely on the way you see and understand something. We all tend to assume that *our* perspective is the *right* perspective. When left with a choice, we naturally trust our own perception and reasoning as being truthful. We trust that deep inside we're being honest with ourselves, but believe it or not, this isn't always the case.

It's possible for you to deceive yourself. Sound crazy? Maybe, but it's true. It's actually possible for your heart to mislead you, to lie to you, to misguide you. James teaches in James 1:14 that *"every man is tempted when he is drawn away of his own lust...."* In this case, we draw *ourselves* away from the right path. We lead *ourselves* into danger. We bring *ourselves* into sin and pain.

Paul taught in Romans 7 that there was a war going on within himself. This war was between his righteous desires and his sinful flesh—or the new man and the old man. Even though he wanted to do right, he often found himself being led astray by his sinful flesh. Apparently this struggle was quite frustrating for him, and he concludes the chapter by crying out *"who shall deliver me...?"* His answer is found in the next verse when he says *"I thank God, through Jesus Christ...."*

The principle is the same in each of these passages. There is a part of all of us that can actually lead us away and deceive us into danger and sin. It was this struggle in Paul that caused him to completely abandon himself to the power of Christ. In Galatians 2:20 he said, *"I am crucified with Christ: nevertheless I live; yet not I, but Christ liveth in me: and the life which I now live in the flesh I live by the faith of the Son of God, who loved me, and gave himself for me."*

Emotions were never meant to be trusted. They were given to us by God to season life's moments with feeling, but they make terrible guides because much of the time they just don't tell the truth. Yet many people base their decisions on emotions; they trust themselves, and they make life-long mistakes based on the misinformation of the moment!

I know teen girls who have fallen in love with and married the wrong guy. Everyone knew it. It was an obvious mistake, but they were closed to anyone's opinion but their own. They were trusting themselves alone! In this type of situation, friends and family have really only one choice— grin and bear it. Very few people, especially parents, would take an opposing side when a child is making a grave mistake. Every parent wants to be thought of as supportive, so usually they smile silently, hoping that somehow everything will work out. Unfortunately, things rarely do just "work out."

In this case, the girl has been blinded by emotion and cannot see reality. Usually just a few short months or years into this type of marriage, reality hits hard (sometimes literally), and one or both partners are running for their lives with broken hearts.

Who do they run to? It never fails, they always go running back to the people they wouldn't listen to in the first place. These are the people that were there all the time (even though their wisdom was silenced), and they always will be there to love and restore a broken life.

Trusting self is always a very dangerous path. It never works out. It's so easy to follow emotion or feeling. It's so easy to rely on your own understanding, which always seems so true and real. It's natural to rely on the way you see things, but it's also deadly.

As a side note on this thing of emotion, remember this: Feelings will always follow obedience. Emotions will always fall in line with reality eventually. There will be times in your life when your emotions are way out of whack, maybe during a hard break up, a personal failure, or a time of trial. During these times, you must determine to cling to what you know to be true—God and His Word. And in time, your emotions will settle back down and fall in line with reality.

Don't run away, kill yourself, or freak out on drugs…no matter the despair that your emotions may bring. Remind yourself that these are just emotions talking, and that there's something greater than emotion—TRUTH. This is what God says about it in 1 John 3:20, *"For if our heart condemn us,* **God is greater than our heart***, and knoweth all things."*

As you obey God, your emotions will eventually catch up, and you'll be glad you listened to the steadfast voice of truth rather than the unstable voice of emotion.

When you put yourself in the prideful position of needing to prove your own self-reliance, you're headed for the "Mistake Zone" every time!

IV. Putting your trust to the test

So how do you know for sure whether you're trusting yourself or God? How can you test your trust?

Let me encourage you to do a little assignment that will help you put this command into practice. Take a few moments at the end of this chapter and get some blank paper and a pen. Find a quiet spot and write these words at the top of the paper—"The Way I See It" (my own understanding).

Then, begin to write out your best description of how you think your life should unfold. Don't play mind games with yourself; just write what comes to mind. Describe things the way you envision them. Be specific. Be transparent.

Be honest. Dream big. Hope for the best. Be realistic. Don't just think it—actually write it down. It won't take that long. What college do you want to attend? Who do you want to marry (or what kind of person)? Where would you like to live, and what would you dream of doing? What kind of house would you like? How many kids? Even write down the things that you believe are "God's will" for your life.

Teaching Tip:
Bring some paper to class and consider spending some time in class actually having your students write out their future plans. If not, at least encourage them to do this assignment at home and bring it back to you. Not all of the students will do it, but the ones who do will greatly benefit from it. You will enjoy reading their plans. Encourage them to follow through with the assignment and to refuse to trust the way they see the future.

There's probably more of this stuff under the surface of your heart than you realize. You might be amazed how much you actually do write down in just a few moments. It might surprise you that you've thought of all this but never quite so clearly. I've had many teens share with me that this experience was one they will never forget! So, be sure to do it.

Once it's all out on paper, read it. Take a good long look at it, like when you're saying goodbye to a friend that you won't see for a long, long time. Savor the moment. Read it a few times, and then find a big red marker and write these words boldly across the page. DO NOT TRUST THIS!

Now realize—it's not necessarily that what you wrote is wrong for your future. It may not be right either. Simply put, it's your own understanding, and you must not trust it for now. This is the best way to articulate from your own heart what the Bible means by the phrase *"thine own understanding"* as stated in Proverbs 3:5–6. It's the way you see things, and it is exactly what the Bible tells you not to trust or lean on.

In order for your future decisions to be right in God's eternal plan, they must be based on faith, and they must come from Him, not yourself. In order to fully lean upon Him, you must come to a release point of your own understanding. You must come to that moment when you consciously decide that you don't trust YOU!

Strange isn't it? All your young adult life you've wanted people to trust you, now I'm telling you not even to trust yourself. Actually, God is telling you from the Bible…I'm just reminding you.

Finally, let me encourage you to seek God's help in making one more change in the years ahead.

Wouldn't it be great if, over time, you could just get in the habit of "leaning to God's understanding" rather than your own. It's natural for all of us to lean to our own; but I believe, over time, God can help you change this natural tendency. I believe every Christian's first thought in any situation should be, "Lord, what is your understanding of this situation?"

Whether it's your next meal or your next major decision, ask the Lord to help you develop the habit of instantly thinking of His way before your own. First Corinthians 10:31 says it this way, *"Whether therefore ye eat, or drink, or whatsoever ye do, **do all to the glory of God.**"*

By the way, save that sheet of paper. You might even need to hang it somewhere prominent to remind yourself what not to trust. You might turn around thirty years from now and be pleasantly surprised at how much of it God brought to pass. You might turn around thirty years from now and be happy that none of it came true. Either way, thirty years from now, you'll want to know that you're living your destiny; and you'll never get there by trusting yourself or leaning to your own understanding.

And don't forget, when you're in the "Mistake Zone," trusting yourself is about as obvious as wearing your pants backwards—at least to those older than you. It really looks pretty goofy!

"Thou wilt keep him in perfect peace, whose mind is stayed on thee: because he trusteth in thee."—Isaiah 26:3

Discussion Questions

1. What are some problems with trusting self?
2. List the three characteristics of people who make right decisions.
3. How can you deceive yourself?
4. What can keep you from trusting the guidance of God's Word?
5. Why is trusting yourself directly defiant towards God?
6. Describe some of your own weaknesses and why it is important that you trust God with them.
7. How can emotions deceive you?
8. On a separate sheet of paper, follow the steps listed under "Putting your trust to the test" in the lesson outline.

Memory Verse

"Thou wilt keep him in perfect peace, whose mind is stayed on thee: because he trusteth in thee."—Isaiah 26:3

Lesson Notes

_____

_____

_____

_____

_____

_____

_____

_____

_____

_____

_____

_____

_____

_____

_____

_____

_____

_____

_____

_____

_____

_____

_____

_____

_____

_____

_____

_____

_____

_____

_____

_____

Lesson Notes

_____

_____

_____

_____

_____

_____

_____

_____

_____

_____

_____

_____

_____

_____

_____

_____

_____

_____

_____

_____

_____

_____

Dimples, Donuts, and Destiny

Step #2—Seek and Surrender to God's Will

Text

"But seek ye first the kingdom of God, and his righteousness; and all these things shall be added unto you."—Matthew 6:33

"I beseech you therefore, brethren, by the mercies of God, that ye present your bodies a living sacrifice, holy, acceptable unto God, which is your reasonable service. And be not conformed to this world: but be ye transformed by the renewing of your mind, that ye may prove what is that good, and acceptable, and perfect, will of God."—Romans 12:1–2

"Thus saith the LORD, the God of Israel; Like these good figs, so will I acknowledge them that are carried away captive of Judah, whom I have sent out of this place into the land of the Chaldeans for their good. For I will set mine eyes upon them for good, and I will bring them again to this land: and I will build them, and not pull them down; and I will plant them, and not pluck them up. And I will give them an heart to know me, that I am the LORD: and they shall be my people, and I will be their God: for they shall return unto me with their whole heart." —Jeremiah 24:5–7

Lesson Aim

This lesson is designed to encourage your students to seek God's perfect will above all other earthly pursuits, and to surrender to it completely before they know what it is. This lesson can be easily divided into two parts.

Teaching Outline

I. Why do some people resist God's will?
   A. It is vague.
   B. It seems to be a threat to your dreams.
   C. It can be a frustrating quest.
   D. We do not understand how good God's plans are.

II. What is God's will? (Jeremiah 24:5–7)
   A. God's will is good.
   B. God's will is His plan to bless you. (Psalm 16:11)
   C. God's will is His plan to lead you and guide you in life. (Psalm 23)
   D. God's will is His plan to provide for you.
   E. God's will is His plan to give you true success.
   F. God's will is never painless or problem free.
   G. God's will is never effortless or easy.
   H. God's will is the only path to full and abundant joy in life.
   I. God's will brings purpose to every trial in your life.
   J. God's will brings provision to every need in your life.
   K. God's will is the only path to a life with no regrets.

III. How does God reveal His will?
   A. God always reveals His will. (Psalm 32:8)
   B. God reveals His will in bite-size pieces.
   C. God reveals His will by faith. (2 Timothy 1:7)

D. God only leads those with willing hearts.

E. God promises to lead you into His will.

F. God's condition is that you must be lead-able.

G. If you are lead-able, God promises to guide you.

IV. Seek God's will first.

A. God commands you to seek Him.

B. God rewards those who seek Him. (Hebrews 11:6)

C. God leads those who seek Him. (Matthew 6:33)

D. God is pleased by those who seek Him.

E. Seeking God's will means God is your first priority.

V. How should a person seek God?

A. Read, study, and meditate on the Bible.

B. Walk with God in prayer.

C. Make church a priority.

D. Read good books and biographies.

E. Listen to godly music.

F. Deliberately separate from worldly influences.

VI. Surrender to God's will completely.

A. You must choose to do God's will before you understand it.

B. God will reveal His will to those who choose to do it first.

C. Complete surrender to God's will is reasonable Christianity. (Romans 12:1–2; 1 Corinthians 6:19–20)

twelve

Dimples, Donuts, and Destiny
Step #2—Seek and Surrender to God's Will

I. Why do some people resist God's will?

God's will. Those words echo so often in the halls of a Bible-believing church or school. If you've grown up in a Christian home you've heard them all of your life. Those two words are so mysterious, so intangible, so hard to grasp. What is it? Why is it? How does it affect my life today? How do I find it? When will I know I've found it? What will it be like? What if I don't like it?

All these questions make a fairly simple issue so complex and intricate that many young adults have one of three negative reactions to it.

First, this vague concept, "God's will" seems so intangible that we just give up trying to understand it—let alone seek it or surrender to it. Out of sheer ignorance, we miss God's best simply because we "don't understand it." This boils down to self-centered rebellion.

Secondly, this "will" (whatever it is) seems to threaten our hopes and dreams, so we run from it as fast as we can (another path of rebellion). We don't want "God's will" to ruin our lives and shatter all of those well-laid plans we talked about earlier.

Thirdly, those of a spiritual mindset can begin weaving an intricate maze of mental questions, theories, and personal puzzles that lead them in frustrating circles of thought. They wonder what is God's will? They theorize if it's this or that. They exhaust themselves, entertaining a myriad of possibilities. They jump to radical conclusions for weird reasons. It's like a psychotic Easter egg hunt…and we're not finding any eggs! This circular reasoning drives us spiritually insane with this question—"What is God up to and why won't He tell me?"

This response feels like a desperate "spiritual quest," but in reality it is exhausting, frustrating, and can often lead to depression, despair, and even spiritual failure. This self-centered quest can easily turn into serious disappointment with God and with the spiritual growth process, which can drive us away from God altogether. Perhaps you can identify.

Simply put, people who resist God's will or who deliberately reject it just don't understand what it is. Similarly, people who reject God simply don't understand who He is and what He is like. People run from God because they perceive Him to be a threat rather than a Saviour. They believe Him to be a tyrant rather than a loving Father.

Even so, people who resist God's perfect will in their lives have the same condition. They believe the lie that His will is a danger to their desires. They think of God's will as a terrible detour to their personal dreams. They fear that if they seek or surrender to God's will, He will surely send them to some far corner of the globe to eat bugs and to be killed by cannibals.

Regardless of whether I give up on God's will because of ignorance, perceived threat, or sheer frustration—it all boils down to a decision to rebel against God. Resisting God's will is a sheer act of defiance against Almighty God—regardless of my reasons. Rather than trust Him by faith, I choose to rebel. I choose to fight back—to protect my "turf" from God's encroachment.

In short, people resist God's will by choice—because they do not understand that His will is better than they could ever imagine.

Think of it this way—God's perfect will compared to your selfish will is like Disneyland compared to your local mini-golf. One is so blatantly better than the other that the comparison is ludicrous! There really is no comparison. God is our loving Heavenly Father, and He has spent an eternity conceiving a master plan for our lives (destiny). We are the children in the back seat of life with scarcely the ability to imagine what God might have in store.

> **Teaching Tip:**
> Students often fear God's will. Consider using a birthday present or Christmas gift as an illustration. Nobody is afraid of opening a birthday present or Christmas gift, so why do we fear God's will? You can develop this in a number of ways. Be creative, and encourage them to view God's will as a gift, not a threat.

God offers us a "surprise" (by faith) plan that He knows we're going to love, if we just trust Him. The moment we fully understand His plan we're going to thank Him for all of eternity. But we're demanding, arrogant, and ignorant. Beyond that, we're clinging to our feeble and meager plans as though we're holding the exclusive recipe for happiness and success.

There we sit in the back seat, arms folded, frowning, demanding our way. In childlike ignorance we refuse to trust the Father and wait out His timing. All the while, God is offering us a perfect will that far exceeds and surpasses the selfish ways for which we fight.

II. What is God's will?

"Thus saith the LORD, the God of Israel; Like these good figs, so will I acknowledge them that are carried away captive of Judah, whom I have sent out of this place into the land of the Chaldeans for their good. For I will set mine eyes upon them for good, and I will bring them again to this land: and I will build them, and not pull them down; and I will plant them, and not pluck them up. And I will give them an heart to know me, that I am the LORD: and they shall be my people, and I will be their God: for they shall return unto me with their whole heart."
—Jeremiah 24:5–7

In this passage, God is describing His plans or His will for His people. These verses uniquely show God's awesome heart of compassion and goodness. Notice that God says, *"so will I acknowledge them"* indicating that He knows, recognizes, and is interested in His people. He acknowledges you, right now!

Then He says, *"I will set mine eyes upon them for good,"* showing that His plans are always good and working for eternal good. This means God isn't planning to ruin your life! He has good things in mind for your future! Have you ever considered the fact that God likes you and that He has good plans for your life?

He goes on to describe His plan to lead His people, build them, plant them, and fellowship with them. What an awesome, loving Heavenly Father we have! It's humbling to think that the Creator of the universe would go to such detail in His feelings, thoughts, and plans for each of us!

What is His will? Well, I cannot tell you the specific details of His plans, but I can tell you His promise. He promises that His will is good. He promises that He will lead you. He promises that He will provide for you and bless you with true success.

Simply, God's will is the daily unfolding of your life as designed by the perfect, infinite, loving, awesome mind of God. It's so wonderful you cannot imagine it. It's so joyful, that the psalmist simply said, *"Thou wilt shew me the path of life: in thy presence is fulness of joy; at thy right hand there are pleasures for evermore"* (Psalm 16:11). It's so intricate that you can only take it in "daily doses." It's so right that once you experience it, you'll never look back.

It isn't problem free, carefree, or painless. It isn't easy, effortless, or lighthearted. Sometimes it's uphill. Sometimes it involves tears or trials. Sometimes it leads through valleys. Sometimes it involves burdens or disappointments. But life in general includes all of that as well—without the promises of God attached.

God's will isn't some rosy life of bliss and blessings. God never promises a perfect, problem-free path. His will includes a vast array of life experiences that range from the pleasant to the painful—and everywhere in between.

The difference between God's will and your own is this. Your will might provide temporary joy from time to time— His will provides fullness of joy. Your will might lead through painful experiences that you must face alone—His will provides strength, provision, security, and love during painful experiences that He foreordains. In addition to this, through every trial, in His will, you'll have the sustaining peace that He is there; He is in control; He is carrying you through; and

He is weaving something good in your life. Your own will offers no such promise.

Living in your own will leads you to a lonely, barren place where you must be your own god. You must provide for yourself, sustain yourself, and depend upon yourself. In the face of tragedy, job-loss, or disaster, you are alone; and you are forced to find your own solution. Something impossible for mere "sheep."

In God's will, whether on a mountain top or in a valley, you can rest in knowing that God is leading you, and your soul *"shall not want"* (Psalm 23). In God's will you will find true success, purpose in life, and internal joy. In God's will you can have confidence that even the most mundane details of your day align somehow with God's awesome design! In God's will you will know what life is all about and how you fit into His eternal plan. In God's will, you can pillow your head each night with true peace and satisfaction, and you can face death with confidence. Wherever His will leads you, His grace will sustain you, and His power will keep you.

Finally, from the deathbed of your own will, you will look back regretting a life of bad choices and missed blessings. Yet, from the deathbed of God's will, with a full heart of joy, you will look back on a rich legacy of spiritual blessings with no regrets!

God's will for you is a detailed account of your life, pre-written in eternity past. He will unveil this plan to you moment by moment along your life-journey. At every turn, He already knows what is around the next bend, and He has already provided what you need when you get there. God's will takes you from birth through a series of decisions and choices (both yours and others) leading to the ultimate fulfillment of your purpose for existing. God's will is your life lived by God's leading, for God's glory, and within God's control. It's awesome!

In all of life's desired experiences…God's will is the one experience that you don't want to miss!

III. How does God reveal His will?

So many young adults struggle with the concept of God's will. Some struggle with surrendering to something they cannot see or comprehend. They feel as though they are "leaping in the dark."

Others have no problem surrendering to it, yet they struggle trying to find it or hoping to understand it. They worry needlessly about it and often work themselves into an emotional frenzy trying to reason it out.

A good look at biblical accounts of God's leading in the hearts of His people will help you deal with either of these issues. If you are struggling to surrender, you only need to see that God never fails, never falters, never lies, and never lets you down. This will compel you to surrender and give you confidence that His will truly is the "only option."

If you are struggling with finding it, needing to know it, or worrying about it; you'll find in Scripture that God always reveals His will in "bite-size" pieces. Think of the stories we've already talked about—Moses, Abraham, Joseph, Peter, etc. God led all of these individuals one *nerve-racking* step at a time! (Emphasis on *nerve-racking*!) There's not one person who knew the whole story up-front. There's not even one person that knew *some* of the story up-front. They were all led one step at a time, one moment at a time…but don't let this escape your realization. They *were* led! God has never failed to lead *one* of His followers!

The key is they were all listening! They all had listening hearts and ready minds. They were all surrendered and ready to follow His lead. They knew how to walk with Him, wait on Him, trust in Him, and recognize His hand at work. We'll talk more about that in a coming chapter, but for now, take note—God never fails to lead those who are of willing hearts! He wants to! He's waiting to! He *will!*

Perhaps you have been searching, worrying, and even panicking over finding God's will. Relax! If you are willing and surrendered, He will guide you! He won't let you make a wrong move (Psalm 32:8). He's not hiding it from you. Just wait on Him, seek Him, and in His time everything will fall into place.

Perhaps it drives you crazy that you cannot see more than a "few steps" down the path. Relax. That's how God works. So long as you know you're following Him, what does it matter? He sees tomorrow, He knows the future, and you'll get there in His time. Worrying about it, stewing over it, and working yourself into a frenzy serves only to rob your joy and minimize your trust.

Second Timothy 1:7 tells us, *"For God hath not given us the **spirit of fear**; but of power, and of love, and of a sound mind."* If you are fearful or anxious about not knowing God's will, perhaps you're not really living by faith. True faith will rest in God's good promise and truly trust Him with the future.

Think of it this way. It's not up to you to *find* His will as much as it's up to Him to *lead* you into it. Your primary responsibility is to be *lead-able*—to stay soft, sensitive, surrendered, and right with Him so that He can guide you day by day.

When I was in my later high school years, this was my big fear. I didn't want to miss His will. I didn't want to end up on my deathbed having taken too many wrong turns. The thought literally scared me.

Surely, you *can* miss God's will for your life, but the question is how? In Psalm 32:8, God taught me that missing His will was more related to me denying His leading than it was to me missing His clues.

I had this mental picture that God had created a perfect will, hidden it among all the other options of life, and then sent me out into young adulthood to find it for myself. My idea was that it was a scavenger hunt for my destiny, and I was truly hoping to find it. I was afraid of missing it.

The promise in Psalm 32:8 taught me that there is NO WAY for a *surrendered* person to miss God's will, apart from God breaking His promise. (That's impossible!) He has promised to lead you and guide you, so long as you are lead-able. He says in verse nine, *"Be ye not as the horse, or as the mule, which have no understanding...."* In other words, if you choose to resist, if you choose not to be led, like a stubborn mule or horse, you *will* miss it. So, God says, "don't be that way!"

If you're spending a great deal of time worrying about God's will—stop. Focus more on drawing close to Him, walking with Him, and knowing Him. Concentrate on having a surrendered heart. Consume yourself with being lead-able, and God will take care of everything else.

IV. Seek God's will first

There is a difference between seeking God's will and fretting over it. Hebrews 11:6 tells us that God rewards those who diligently seek Him. Matthew 6:33 tells us to seek first the kingdom of God. Other verses command us to draw nigh to Him, seek Him early, and give Him first priority in our lives. Obviously God wants us to seek Him, to seek His will, and to make His kingdom the primary pursuit of our lives. In light of these Scriptures, when it comes to God's will, I challenge you to begin seeking!

By now, hopefully you recognize that God's will is wonderful! It is not something to fear, but it is something to anticipate! It is not something to run from but to run to! It is not something that threatens our futures, but rather holds our futures. Hopefully, by now, you want God's will!

I firmly believe that God is pleased when His people seek Him and seek His ways. I believe He delights when we choose to pursue Him, to know Him, to understand Him, to learn of Him. I believe that He reveals Himself most fully and intimately to those who truly seek Him personally.

If God's will is something you desire, then you should begin communicating that desire to God through a seeking heart. You should begin deliberately studying, praying, and meditating on truths that teach you of God's will and ways. Begin a quest for God and for His truth. At this point, it should not merely be a self-centered, need-to-know the details quest. It's far deeper and richer than that. This is a quest to walk with, to understand, and to know the heart and mind of God.

Think of it this way. Right now, in your life, you are seeking something. It may be something intangible like acceptance, friendships, popularity, or prestige. It may be something tangible like a car, a job, a driver's license, or a status symbol. Chances are you woke up this morning with something on your heart and mind—something you are seeking. It may be a dating relationship with some special person, a grade point average in a certain course, or a promotion at work. What are you seeking?

I submit to you, based upon the Scriptures, if God's will is something that you really desire, you must seek it *first*, above all else. This might seem like a high-hurdle for you to get over at this point in life, but you must. If God's will is not your first priority, it may as well be your last. You'll never experience it.

Seek God's will first above every pursuit and desire of your heart. Make Him preeminent. Make His plans your priority. Show him, in your seeking, that you are hungry to know Him and to follow Him every step of the way. In so doing, you will not only please Him greatly, you will know Him personally.

V. How should a person seek God?

There are many ways to seek God and His will, but here are a few practical ways that you could begin seeking Him right now:

A. Read, study, and meditate on the Bible

Do character studies, word studies, or topical searches on following God and knowing God. Study how Bible characters followed Him. Study those who rebelled. Read everything in Scripture that you can find about God's leading and God's will.

B. Walk with God in prayer

Take a walk with God literally. Sometimes it's hard to stay awake if you pray kneeling or in bed. Get up a few minutes earlier and take a walk around the block before school. Slip out of the house at sunset and walk the neighborhood. While you do, talk to God. Give Him your undivided attention and ask Him the questions

that are on your heart. Communicate your true desires
and thoughts to Him.

C. Make church a priority

It's a priority with God, so it should be with you too.
If church is unimportant to you, then so is God's will.
Don't work on Sundays. Go to church and listen with
an open heart to every lesson, every song, and every
message. You'll be surprised how much God will address
your specific questions or thoughts during these times if
you have an open and seeking heart.

D. Read good books and biographies

Ask godly mentors in your life what books they've read
that have impacted them greatly. Read biographies of
great Christians who walked with God. Read books
about spiritual maturity and growth. All of these
resources will equip you for the journey ahead and
mature you in God's grace. Each tool will be useful in
the hands of the Holy Spirit as He speaks to your heart
and molds you for God's glory.

E. Listen to godly music

Godly music will lift your heart towards the Lord. It will
motivate you to love Him and to listen to Him more
attentively. This kind of music will nourish your soul
and sharpen your mind. God will use it to lead you
forward in your spiritual journey.

F. Deliberately separate from worldly influences

We've talked about a pure heart, but think of it this way. Each worldly influence serves to deaden your spiritual senses and dull your understanding. At this time in your life, you need every spiritual insight that you can get. Get rid of things that take your heart away from spiritual things.

There are probably many other ways, but this is a start. If you want to live God's will day by day, then you must begin seeking God as your first priority in life. Truly, He's the only One worthy of that preeminence!

VI. Surrender to God's will completely

Question: Why should God feel obligated to reveal His will to someone who has no intention of following it? Answer: He shouldn't. Fact: He won't.

So, let me cut you off at the pass. If you have the intention of *seeking* His will and then determining *if* you will do it or not, forget it. You cannot choose to do His will *after* you see what it is. This choice must be made before He will ever reveal it to you. That's what faith is all about. God doesn't make deals. He knows your heart before you ever begin seeking. If you are seeking His will with ulterior motives, God won't play that game.

It's not about finding out what God wants to do with your life. It's about choosing God and knowing that *He* is enough. It's about knowing that He is your life and your only hope of true success and happiness. When you make that realization, you'll choose Him, and His plan will simply become a by-product of your intimate walk with Him. At that point, you won't need to know *what* He wants you to do.

You'll just be glad to know He's yours and you're His…and everything else will be just fine!

"I beseech you therefore, brethren, by the mercies of God, that ye present your bodies a living sacrifice, holy, acceptable unto God, which is your reasonable service. And be not conformed to this world: but be ye transformed by the renewing of your mind, that ye may prove what is that good, and acceptable, and perfect, will of God."—Romans 12:1–2

God expects unconditional surrender prior to revealing His will. In His economy, this kind of surrender is reasonable. He expects you to sign a blank sheet of paper so that He can fill in the details. He is looking for complete abandon and total trust.

You might be thinking, "Are you kidding? God expects me to just abandon everything *before* I even know what He's going to have me do?"

Exactly. That's what the disciples did when Jesus said, "Follow me." That's what Abraham did when God said, "Leave your homeland." That's what Joseph did when God said, "Go to jail. Go directly to jail." That's what Mary did when God said, "Surprise, you're expecting!" That's what every great Bible character did at some point in life. They abandoned themselves in total surrender to God's plan. They truly loved God more than anything or anyone else!

This is directly opposed to what your social science teacher will tell you. You won't get this advice from your public school guidance counselor. You won't find it on *Oprah*, and it won't be featured in *Seventeen* magazine or in any other worldly resource. It's still true. It's still the right way to live.

Simply put, God will not guide you or lead you until He knows that you are fully surrendered to Him.

Have you ever come to that vital moment when you knelt down and completely gave your life to God? If not, now is the time. What's holding you back? What is it about God that you don't trust? What are you afraid of? Why do you feel that God is such a threat?

Face that fear. Call it what it is—faithless defiance. Call it distrust. Call it an accusation that God is not truthful or faithful. Call it pride and arrogance. At the very least, call it a lie that you should stop believing. Then let go—surrender. It's not hard. It's not some impenetrable fortress. It's just a choice.

Bow down on your knees; confess to God that He is everything He claims; and then surrender completely to His every desire. Tell Him you will do whatever He wants you to do. Tell Him you will follow wherever He leads and obey whatever He says. Tell Him you belong completely to Him… it's your "reasonable service."

You are not your own (1 Corinthians 6:19–20). You were bought with the blood of Jesus Christ, and you exist for the purpose and glory of Almighty God. Give God what is rightly His and stop laying claim on His purchased possession—your life.

There is sweetness in surrender that touches the deepest reaches of our beings. There is deep, incomparable joy in letting God have control. There is an intimate and consuming peace that passes all understanding when you finally reach the point of giving in.

When you completely surrender to God's will, not knowing what it is, you are truly expressing a very genuine faith, and you are on a collision course with destiny!

One final thought about God's will. God will not force His will on you. He doesn't force Himself on anybody. He has always given man a free will in matters relating to eternity. Even Jonah, though relentlessly pursued by God, had a choice. You must choose Him. You must seek Him and surrender to Him. You must initiate the process of surrender, and He will most definitely respond.

My children take great delight when I announce to them that I have a surprise planned! They cheer, they jump up and down, they anticipate my plans with great animation! Do you think we could be that way with God? Do you think we could explode with joyful anticipation at the mere mention of His good and perfect will for us? Do you think we could celebrate His plan, even though we don't know what it is? Do you think we could be that childish? I sure hope so. Something tells me that would make God very, very happy.

So, while you're chewing on all this "God's will" stuff, mainly remember to sit back, relax, and know that you're going to have a great life so long as God is planning it.

"Blessed is every one that feareth the LORD; that walketh in his ways."—Psalm 128:1

Discussion Questions

1. Why do some people resist God's will?
2. How does God reveal His will?
3. How does God respond towards those who seek Him?
4. What is reasonable Christianity?
5. List some promises of doing God's will that you hope to see fulfilled in your own life.
6. Describe some of the struggles you may face if you choose God's will, but explain why the struggles would be worth it.
7. What does it mean to be "lead-able," and how can you become a more "lead-able" person?
8. What are you currently doing to seek God? Name one other thing that you will do this week to help you seek God.

Memory Verse

"Blessed is every one that feareth the LORD; that walketh in his ways."—Psalm 128:1

Lesson Notes

_____

_____

_____

_____

_____

_____

_____

_____

_____

_____

_____

_____

_____

_____

_____

_____

_____

_____

_____

_____

_____

_____

_____

_____

Speak Up, God, I Can't Hear You!

Step #3—Pray About Your Decision

Text

"Pray without ceasing."—1 Thessalonians 5:17

"The wicked, through the pride of his countenance, will not seek after God: God is not in all his thoughts."—Psalm 10:4

"For God speaketh once, yea twice, yet man perceiveth it not." —Job 33:14

"And the LORD called Samuel again the third time. And he arose and went to Eli, and said, Here am I; for thou didst call me. And Eli perceived that the LORD had called the child." —1 Samuel 3:8

Lesson Aim

The purpose of this lesson is to help young people understand how God speaks to His children and how prayer plays a part in the decision-making process. In this lesson, students will understand that God speaks with a still, small voice, and He must be carefully sought out and listened to. They will be challenged to silence the other voices in their world so that they can hear and follow God's voice alone.

Teaching Outline

I. Silencing the voices from without
    A. We are all faced with many opportunities in life.
    B. Each opportunity could potentially draw us away from God's will.
    C. The voices of these opportunities must be silenced through surrender.
    D. If we listen to the voices of selfish opportunities, we cannot hear God's voice.

II. Understanding how God speaks to His children (2 Kings 19:9–15)
    A. God will never force Himself upon you.
    B. God is always speaking.
    C. God speaks through His Word.
    D. God speaks through our circumstances.
    E. God speaks with His still small voice within.
    F. God only speaks to listening hearts. (Job 33:14; 1 Samuel 3:8)
    G. Listening to God's voice in your heart is different from "following your heart."

III. Feigning prayer to soothe the conscience
    A. It is possible to fake prayer to soothe the conscience.
    B. Fake prayer always begins with an unsurrendered heart.
    C. Fake prayer will make you feel better about rebellion.
    D. Fake prayer becomes a cover up for wrong decisions.

IV. How to pray about decisions (1 Thessalonians 5:17)
   A. God is interested in a moment-by-moment, personal relationship with you. (Psalm 10:5; Genesis 5)
   B. Prayer is as simple as capturing your thoughts and directing them toward God.
   C. Prayer should begin with adoration.
   D. Prayer should continue with confession. (Psalm 51)
   E. Prayer should continue with thanksgiving.
   F. Prayer should conclude with supplication.
   G. Consider keeping a prayer journal.

thirteen

Lesson Thirteen
Speak Up, God, I Can't Hear You!
Step #3—Pray About Your Decision

Once you've come to a point of total surrender to God's
unseen will, you are ready to begin seriously **praying** about
your decision. How do you pray? Why pray? What happens
when you pray? What will God do in response to your
prayer? What are you hoping to get through prayer? All of
these questions will be addressed in the next few pages, so
stay with me.

I. Silencing the voices from without

Imagine that you are standing in a room called "life" and
there are four people standing around you—one in front,
one behind, and one on either side of you. For the sake of
illustration, these people will represent four opportunities for

your future. For now we'll just call them "voices." These four people represent things you could do, opportunities that will open up to you, and influences that will try to persuade you to choose one way or another.

The first person in front of you is the person you might date or fall in love with. Imagine that he or she is standing directly in front of you talking loudly about plans for your future. This person will represent voice #1.

Now, let's imagine that the person behind you represents your current employer. For the sake of illustration, let's assume that for the past two years you've worked at Wendy's hamburger restaurant. You've become an expert at flipping burgers, frying French fries, and pouring large Frosties. In fact, you've done so well, management has promoted you. They like you. They would love to keep you on the Wendy's team and make you a permanent part of their organization. Imagine that this man is promising you further training, management promotions, and higher pay in your present job. He represents voice #2.

With one person in front of you talking loudly and one person behind you talking loudly, the person to your left starts shouting too, trying to be heard over the other voices.

For the sake of being absurd, let's imagine that one of your highly acclaimed skills is ballet. (C'mon...work with me here.) Let's imagine that ever since you were little, you excelled at ballet. In fact, you have become one of the finest ballerinas or balladeers in the nation. (The guys in my Sunday school class really cringe when I use them for this illustration.)

To your left stands a representative of the New York Ballet. He is offering you a highly acclaimed position. He is loudly promising you a high salary, worldwide fame, and a host of other incentives. He is compelling you to come and join his award-winning team of ballet professionals. In fact, imagine that he has grabbed your arm and is forcefully trying to pull you in his direction.

To your right is a representative of the University of California in Los Angeles (UCLA). This man is here to offer you a full four-year scholarship for a pre-med degree from UCLA with the promise of medical school, residency, and a lucrative practice in the years to come. He is loudly shouting and touting his offer, trying to convince you to choose his school, and he too has grabbed your arm and is actively pulling you his direction.

There you stand, surrounded with *promising* opportunities. By the way, you don't have to go along with my absurd illustrations. You could fill in the blank faces with whatever opportunities are currently trying to persuade or pull you in a direction. You could fill in the blanks with whatever your interests, hobbies, or academic skills lend themselves to.

These four (or more) voices are now shouting loudly, competing with each other for your future, pulling for you to move their direction, and actively trying to recruit you. It's confusing. It's loud. It's frustrating. It's a very difficult choice.

This is where you will be—sooner or later. You will have opportunities. You will face these voices in one form or another. The faces will be different, but they will be there trying to pull you, to monopolize your attention, and influence your future. You will have job offers, college offers, and relational opportunities; and these "promising opportunities" will come your way when you least expect them. Most importantly, they will attempt to confuse your decision-making process, and you must be prepared for them.

By the way, these voices may not all be wrong or sinful. In fact, eventually God's calling for your life will come in this same way—as an opportunity. I'm not saying that every voice is wrong. I'm just calling your attention to the fact that every opportunity has a voice, and many times those voices drown out God's voice.

Imagine that, outside of the circle of voices that has surrounded you stands your Heavenly Father. He's not speaking, shouting, or pulling. He's not a part of the chaos. He's just waiting. He's waiting for you. He waits patiently and silently.

Having seen Him and recognized Him—imagine that you deliberately look at voice #1, and you silence it. You intentionally turn a deaf ear to the demands of this person you're dating. Then you forcefully pull your arms from the grasps of voices #3 and #4 and turn a deaf ear to them as well. You're letting go of these opportunities. You're making a conscious effort to silence their influence in your heart, for the moment.

Finally, you turn and face Wendy's (voice #2) and deliberately still that voice as well. Now, all the voices are quiet, all of the opportunities have been put on hold, and you stand alone in silence.

This is a picture of surrender. Now it's just you and God, standing in an empty room called life…and He's standing there waiting for you.

At this point, you move to where God is, you kneel down before His presence, and you begin to ask for His guidance and help. You pour your heart out to Him. You rehearse all of the things the voices were shouting at you, asking for His insight and opinion on each opportunity.

You have bowed before His presence with an open heart. You're not clinging to any single hope or dream. You are empty handed—having truly let go of all the things that were calling for your life. Now, you're finally ready to begin praying for God's direction.

Until you come to this powerful point of surrender, you're simply not ready to pray for God's guidance. Why should God answer the prayer of a person who isn't really planning on obeying the answer in the first place? Why should God feel obligated to reveal His will to someone who isn't completely committed to following it?

If you're still struggling with this idea of surrender, you should still pray, but your praying should focus on seeking God's help to surrender. In other words, your prayers should say something like "God help me to trust you" or "God give me the courage to surrender to you."

On the other hand, once you finally silence the voices and let go of the opportunities, you are truly ready to bow before God and ask for His guidance and leading.

II. Understanding how God speaks to His children

God will always try to speak to you. So how does God speak?

Primarily, God speaks today through His Word. He doesn't speak audibly, and He doesn't appear in burning bushes or through "weeping" crucifixes. He speaks through the Word of God to your heart. At the same time, He speaks through His indwelling Holy Spirit in your heart. But understand, His still small voice within will always be consistent with the final authority of His preserved Word.

Many people today elevate some personal experience to be equal to the Word of God, but this is a dangerous path.

Even Peter in 2 Peter 1:16–21 declares that the Word of God was "more sure" than his own eyewitness or his own personal experience. While the bulk of this chapter will be about hearing and discerning the voice of God within, you must realize that this "inner guidance" must never come above the authority of God's Word in your life. To truly understand and hear God speaking, you must be in His Word first and foremost.

In 1 Kings 19:9–15, the prophet Elijah experienced God's leading in a very special way. The Bible says, *"And he came thither unto a cave, and lodged there; and, behold, the word of the LORD came to him, and he said unto him, What doest thou here, Elijah? And he said, I have been very jealous for the LORD God of hosts: for the children of Israel have forsaken thy covenant, thrown down thine altars, and slain thy prophets with the sword; and I, even I only, am left; and they seek my life, to take it away. And he said, Go forth, and stand upon the mount before the LORD. And, behold, the LORD passed by, and a great and strong wind rent the mountains, and brake in pieces the rocks before the LORD; but the LORD was not in the wind: and after the wind an earthquake; but the LORD was not in the earthquake: And after the earthquake a fire; but the LORD was not in the fire: and after the fire a still small voice. And it was so, when Elijah heard it, that he wrapped his face in his mantle, and went out, and stood in the entering in of the cave. And, behold, there came a voice unto him, and said, What doest thou here, Elijah? And he said, I have been very jealous for the LORD God of hosts: because the children of Israel have forsaken thy covenant, thrown down thine altars, and slain thy prophets with the sword; and I, even I only, am left; and they seek my life, to take it away. And the LORD said unto him, Go, return on thy way to the wilderness of Damascus: and when thou comest, anoint Hazael to be king over Syria:"*

In this passage we learn something very significant about the leading of God. God doesn't speak through loud voices. He doesn't compete for your attention. He won't try to shout louder or longer than all of the other opportunities in your life.

No…He will simply speak with a still small voice.

You may be wondering, "What does all of this have to do with prayer?"

The answer—"*everything.*" Why pray about your decision? Because God commands you to diligently seek Him! God intends for you to be the initiator of the seeking, and in turn He will respond to your faith. He will speak to your heart. He will indeed lead you, guide you, and impress you through the still small voice of His spirit within your life.

The catch is, if you don't silence the outside voices and seek His voice alone, you will never hear it.

In Mark 6, Jesus deliberately sends His disciples across the sea and directly into a storm. You probably know the story, but there's an interesting detail in verse 48 that many people completely miss. In the middle of the night, Jesus came walking on the water to the frightened disciples, and in verse 48 the Bible says that Jesus *"would have passed by!"* Think about that. He was literally going to pass right by them, if they didn't notice Him and cry out to Him.

In this verse, once again, we see the nature and character of God. He refused to force His help or assistance upon His followers. Yet, when they noticed Him, He immediately talked with them and helped them.

Consider this—Jesus Christ will stand in the shadows of your life, ready to guide and help you. He will not force His will upon you or forcibly require your obedience.

You may be sailing through the middle of a storm of decisions and confusing opportunities. You may be so busy dealing with the mess that you completely miss Him. You may spend the rest of your life trying to calm your own storms and find your own way home. And all the while, Jesus will be there, quietly waiting to come to your side, calm your storm, and guide you to safety in His perfect plan. Will you notice Him? Will you go to Him? Will you seek Him in prayer and listen for His still small voice? He's waiting to speak if you will place yourself in the position of truly listening. Praying about your decision is all about placing yourself in a position where God will speak to your listening heart.

Remember this, God will not line up among all of the other voices in your life and shout to be heard. He will not compete or settle for partial surrender. He doesn't speak that way. He speaks with a still small voice to a surrendered and listening heart.

Many people have never heard this voice; therefore, they cannot identify with it. If you've never come to a point of full surrender and sincere prayer, then you've probably never heard it either.

Yet, if you will silence the voices and come boldly to the throne of grace—something very wonderful will happen. God will speak to your heart.

The Lord is waiting for you to seek Him. He's eager to answer you, and He's ready to speak to your heart. The problem is we rarely acknowledge Him with our questions; therefore, His voice is foreign to our hearts. The other problem is sometimes we're not really willing to hear His answer.

By the way, I'm not saying to listen to your heart above God's Word or to "let your heart guide you." There's a vast difference between following your heart and following God's voice at work in your heart. One is self-centered; the other comes through real surrender and spiritual seeking. One leads to despair while the other leads to blessing. Be careful that you don't confuse the two.

III. Feigning prayer to soothe the conscience

Have you ever known someone who made a bad decision, yet they claimed to have "prayed about it?" People do this all the time. As human beings, we have the unique ability to deceive ourselves, and this is one of the most prevalent ways that young adults do so. The recipe for self-deception goes something like this:

Trust your own desires and emotions and decide you're going to do something. Godly friends and counselors may know that you're making a wrong decision, but disregard their opinions. Think about what you want and just make up your mind. Now, pray. Sure, go ahead and actually ask God if you should follow through with your decision. Pray for a few seconds, a few minutes, or for weeks if you want to. It doesn't matter at this point, because your prayers are useless. They are simply a "prop." God doesn't respond to this kind of prayer, and He doesn't lead this kind of heart—so your prayers only serve two legitimate purposes.

First, they serve to soothe your conscience. Deep within your conscience, you will recognize that you have made up your mind without God and that you've completely disregarded His principles, and "praying" will make you feel better about your rebellion.

Second, they will serve as your defense in the face of godly counselors. You're going to need a spiritual reason for defending what ultimately are *your own selfish desires*. These "prayers" make a great defense against those who would caution you or warn you that something's not right about this decision. You can counter all resistance with those pious words "Well, I've prayed about this, and God has given me a peace about it."

Of course, what you really mean is you've made up your mind, and you've closed your heart to the matter. The "prayer" talk becomes a convenient shroud to cover up your blatant disregard of spiritual principles.

You can use this "prayer" talk to get or do just about anything that comes to mind. I've heard of adults who "prayed" about leaving their spouse to marry someone else. I know young adults who "prayed" about getting out of church to follow some career path. Pregnant girls have "prayed" about getting abortions, young men have "prayed" about being immoral, and rebellious teens have "prayed" about running away from home to live with another parent. It's actually pretty amazing that God has "led" so many people to do so many things in direct opposition to the principles of His Word.

You see, once you set your mind to follow your own path, "prayer" talk is a great way to cover your tracks. After all, who's going to argue with that kind of defense? Hey, if you've prayed about it, what else can anybody else say— right?

Beware of this kind of prayer. It's not real seeking. It's not genuine. It's simply a cover up for a rebellious heart, and it will lead you to a point of utter despair.

IV. How to pray about decisions

In previous lessons we've talked about praying for wisdom, but at this point, I challenge you to begin praying for guidance. Begin asking God to show you His direction and lead you in His perfect will. Let Him know that you desire only His best and remind Him of His promises to guide and direct your paths (Proverbs 3:5–6, Psalm 32:8).

Practically speaking, there are a lot of ways to pray, and sometimes we get psyched out about praying to the point that we do very little of it. Let's face it. It's pretty hard to actually pray on your knees with head bowed and eyes closed for any serious length of time. Maybe I'm more human than you, but it's during these times that my knees hurt, my brain falls asleep, and my thoughts wander. It's often during these times that I'm more focused on the discomfort of my physical position than I am on walking with my wonderful Saviour! (How's that for sheer honesty?)

Now, don't get me wrong. There's also something very scriptural about falling to your knees or on your face in humility and worship before God. You should do this as a regular part of your walk with God. There should be frequent private times when you literally bow before Him in adoration, confession, and thanksgiving. I'm simply saying that the physical obstacles in this often keep us from praying to God at all…because we think that prayer only counts if we're on our knees. It's hard to motivate ourselves to *want* to spend a lot of time in this physical position of prayer.

In addition to this we're commanded in 1 Thessalonians 5:17 to *"pray without ceasing!"* The Bible also says that God wants to be in *"all of our thoughts"* (Psalm 10:4). When you take this into consideration, it becomes obvious that there are ways to pray that don't involve dark closets or difficult physical positions.

Genesis 5 teaches us that Enoch *"walked with God."* Genesis 6 teaches us that Noah *"walked with God."* The Bible is replete with occasions of godly men carrying on their daily, moment-by-moment relationship with God in a very personal and intimate way.

So, let me encourage you to do the same in your prayer life. Make prayer a part of your daily walk, your daily life, and your moment-by-moment thought processes.

Prayer is as simple as thinking. Did it ever occur to you that you are always thinking? Your brain never really stops thinking. The more that you and I can begin capturing those thoughts and directing them to God in prayer, the more we are truly following the teaching of God's Word to *"pray without ceasing"* and to have God in *"all of our thoughts."*

You can pray while you drive, pray in the shower, pray while you get ready in the morning, and pray while you eat breakfast. (It sure beats helping Captain Crunch through the crunch-berry maze on the back of the cereal box for ten minutes every morning!) You can pray while bike riding, exercising, or walking. For me, one of the best ways to pray is to simply take a walk!

There is a multitude of ways to pray, and I encourage you to begin praying in and through everything you do. Make your praying a way of thinking, and specifically pray each and every day that God will guide you moment by moment into His perfect will.

As for *what* to pray, our pastor and others have taught a simple little four-point guide for prayer. Just remember the word ACTS when you pray. The letters stand for the following kinds of prayer:

Adoration—First, spend time adoring and worshipping God for His greatness, power, and love.

Confession—Then, ask Him to bring to mind anything that's not right in your life. Confess sin and make your heart right with Him. Ask Him to cleanse your heart and purify your life (Psalm 51).

Thanksgiving—Spend time thanking God for everything in your life. Thank Him for the blessings and the trials at the same time.

Supplication—Finally, bring your requests to God. Ask Him to help you, mold you, change you, guide you, and lead you. Ask Him to intervene in the special needs on your heart and mind. Bring the requests of friends and family before Him and trust Him to answer these prayers.

That little acronym—ACTS—could be your guide for any personal time of prayer. Adore Him, confess to Him, thank Him, and then bring your supplications.

One final thought—keep a prayer journal. I dare you to write down a list of specific requests with an entry date. Keep the list, pray through it regularly, and then write down the date that any request on your list is answered.

You're going to have a "jaw-dropping" experience about twelve months later. If you will consistently ask God for answers for one solid year, you'll be amazed at the ways He will answer specific prayers in your life over a twelve-month period. This is one of the single greatest "faith-building exercises" that you can do as a young adult.

In conclusion, prayer is a critical "step three" in your decision-making process. First, silence the voices. Then come before God regularly to ask for His guidance and help. Then, simply listen. God will speak to your heart with a crystal clear voice—a still small voice. You will know it is Him, and you will have a very clear understanding of what He wants you to do—at least for the next step on your journey. Remember He will lead you on a "need-to-know" basis. He's never going to unveil the whole thing at once, so don't get your hopes up.

One of the saddest verses in the Bible is Job 33:14, *"For God speaketh once, yea twice, yet man perceiveth it not."*

Wouldn't you dread standing before God only to look back on a life that ignored His still small voice? Imagine the regret that you will have one day to realize that God was trying to speak to you your whole life through, yet you never perceived His voice.

To the contrary, one of the happiest verses in the Bible is the account of Samuel hearing God's voice for the first time as a young boy. First Samuel 3:8 says, *"And the LORD called Samuel again the third time. And he arose and went to Eli, and said, Here am I; for thou didst call me. And Eli perceived that the LORD had called the child."* One of the greatest experiences of the Christian journey is to perceive the voice of God speaking to your heart. Many Christians never hear it because they never silence the "noises" of life long enough to discern it. But for those who will consistently enter into His presence, seek His leading, and listen…God still speaks quite undeniably and clearly.

If you will come to God with a surrendered, listening heart, you too will perceive when He is speaking to you. And believe me…He will!

"For God speaketh once, yea twice, yet man perceiveth it not."—Job 33:14

Discussion Questions

1. How do you silence the "voices from without"?
2. How does God speak to His children?
3. What are the characteristics of fake prayer?
4. What are the characteristics of true prayer?
5. List some opportunities you may have in the future that wouldn't necessarily be wrong, but could draw you away from God's will if you're not careful.
6. Why do you think God doesn't just force you to listen to him?
7. Give an illustration of how and why someone might "fake pray" about a decision.
8. Take a moment and write out your own prayer to God regarding your future or a specific decision.

Memory Verse

"Call unto me, and I will answer thee, and show thee great and mighty things, which thou knowest not."—Jeremiah 33:3

Lesson Notes

Tight Ropes, Safety Nets, and Stupid People

Step #4—Seek Godly Counsel

Text

"Hear counsel, and receive instruction, that thou mayest be wise in thy latter end. There are many devices in a man's heart; nevertheless the counsel of the LORD, that shall stand."
—Proverbs 19:20–21

"Every purpose is established by counsel: and with good advice make war."—Proverbs 20:18

"Blessed is the man that walketh not in the counsel of the ungodly, nor standeth in the way of sinners, nor sitteth in the seat of the scornful."—Psalm 1:1

"Where no counsel is, the people fall: but in the multitude of counsellors there is safety."—Proverbs 11:14

"Without counsel purposes are disappointed: but in the multitude of counsellors they are established."—Proverbs 15:22

"The way of a fool is right in his own eyes: but he that hearkeneth unto counsel is wise."—Proverbs 12:15

"There is no wisdom nor understanding nor counsel against the LORD."—Proverbs 21:30

Lesson Aim

The purpose of this lesson is to help the students understand the value and the importance of godly counsel from God-given authorities in the decision-making process. In this lesson, counsel will be compared to a safety net for a tight-rope walker. This is the step that will prevent a young person from falling into destruction. This lesson could easily be taught over two weeks.

Teaching Outline

I. What do you do after God speaks to you?
  A. You must verify God's leading with a multitude of godly counselors. (Proverbs 20:18)
  B. You must pass a pure heart test by hearing godly counselors.

II. There are two types of counsel. (Psalm 1:1)
  A. Counsel can be godly.
  B. Counsel can be ungodly. (2 Kings 12:3-8; 2 Chronicles 12:14; Proverbs 1:25)

III. Why do you need counsel?
  A. The principle of confirmation (Revelation 2:6; Psalm 1:3)
  B. The principle of God-ordained authority (Hebrews 13:7; Ephesians 6:2; Job 1:10; Ecclesiastes 10:8)
  C. The principle of self-deception

IV. How do you get godly counsel?
  A. Refuse to fake getting counsel.
  B. Refuse to force your counselors to support you.
  C. Have a multitude of godly counselors. (Proverbs 11:14; Proverbs 15:22)

D. Listen with an open heart. (Proverbs 12:15; Proverbs 19:20; Proverbs 20:5)

E. Look for either confirmation or contradiction to your decision.

F. Avoid a "counsel debate."

V. Don't defy a multitude of godly counselors.

A. Don't be afraid to get godly advice.

B. Don't make a decision if a multitude of counselors are not in agreement. (Psalm 33:11)

C. Wait for God to confirm His leading through godly counselors. (Proverbs 21:30)

fourteen

Lesson Fourteen
Tight Ropes, Safety Nets, and Stupid People
Step #4—Seek Godly Counsel

I've heard of people killing themselves in stupid ways—like the guy who pulled a Coke machine over on himself while trying to shake loose a free can of Coke. Or, the lady who broke the law by parachuting over a cliff to prove how "safe it was." She died when her parachute didn't open. People all over the world die for stupid reasons, and tightrope walkers who die without safety nets should be right at the top of the list. The gene pool must not have been kind to this crowd.

Really now, if you're going to choose circus performing at significant heights for a career path; how much training does it take to figure out that you need a safety net? The word *splat* must not mean anything to these people!

I don't feel sorry for circus performers who die stupid deaths without safety nets. Maybe I just don't have the "gift of mercy." Pray for me.

Likewise, I don't feel sorry for young adults who make bad decisions without getting advice either. Godly counsel or "advice" is literally the "safety net" that God has given you to undergird your decisions. It's the "system of checks and balances" to verify that your heart is pure and that your direction is truly biblical. It's the last thing that's going to catch you just before you drop to a "Mistake Zone" of bad choices.

Think of it this way—just in case you've deceived yourself, and you're headed down a dark road with a bridge out, godly counsel is the last warning sign along the road that's going to cause you to turn back. Proverbs 19:21 says, *"There are many devices in a man's heart; nevertheless the counsel of the LORD, that shall stand."*

On the flip side, godly counsel is the final confirmation of God's true leading and direction in your heart. It's His way of proving Himself to you, and it's the safest way to absolutely know for sure that you're doing the right thing.

"Every purpose is established by counsel: and with good advice make war."—Proverbs 20:18

I. What do you do after God speaks to you?

When you finally reach the point of sincere, surrendered prayer, good things are about to happen. God is going to speak to you and lead you. You won't get struck by lightning or see a 500-foot Jesus standing at the end of your bed. You won't feel warm and tingly, and you won't pass out with convulsions.

His leading may not be immediate, but it will be "in time!" In other words, God will speak to you when it's time. Until He does, don't sweat it. For instance, if He hasn't completely confirmed His will for college, that's okay. Don't get uptight about it. Just keep a listening heart. In time, He will confirm His leading in your heart.

This fourth step in decision-making, getting godly counsel, is absolutely one of the most important principles you will read in this entire book. Without it, you are in grave danger. While you can most certainly get counsel at any point in your spiritual growth, this step must absolutely follow the moment that God speaks to your heart. In other words, in between the moment that you hear God's still small voice and the moment that you finalize your decision, you must seek the counsel of godly influences in your life to verify what you believe God has said to you.

The most critical time to get godly counsel in your life is after God has put a direction on your heart—but before you finalize your decision. At this point, you have done everything personally to seek God first, and now you're going to verify God's leading though a "multitude" of counselors.

Remember how I promised you that there is a way to "know for sure" that you're making a right decision? There is a biblical way to know for sure that you're marrying the right person, choosing the right college, and following the right career path. Well, this is the key step in getting that assurance. This is the litmus test of a pure heart, sincere motives, and true Holy Spirit leading. After all that we've learned and studied up to this point, this is the capstone—the final confirmation that you need before you "leap!" If you get anything in this book, get this.

II. There are two types of counsel

In the Bible, the word counsel simply refers to advice or purposes, and the Scriptures are clear that there are two types of counsel—just as there are two types of wisdom. The Bible refers to **godly counsel** and **ungodly counsel**.

Psalm 1:1 says it this way, *"Blessed is the man that walketh not in the counsel of the ungodly, nor standeth in the way of sinners, nor sitteth in the seat of the scornful."*

As you stand at the edge of your next decision, you will be surrounded by both types of counsel—godly and ungodly. There will always be those who try to advise you against God's will and those who try to advise you towards God's will, and it's up to you to choose who you will listen to.

In fact, I know many young adults who "play" ungodly counsel against godly counsel, or those who deliberately choose to hear ungodly counsel because they know they will be told what they want to hear. This kind of "game" is not what the Bible is referring to when it challenges us to get counsel.

Remember this, if you have chosen to follow your own will, it will be very easy to find people who will side with you. Usually it will be your friends—other young adults who don't know any more than you do about life. (Probably less!) They will say things like "It's you're life, do whatever you want" or "Come on, everybody's doing it...."

Here is the key principle—ungodly counsel will always find *you*. Godly counsel is just the opposite—you must find *it*!

In 1 Kings 12:3–8, we read the account of a young king faced with a tough decision. Rehoboam made the mistake of his life in this passage. It reads like this, *"That they sent and called him. And Jeroboam and all the congregation of Israel came, and spake unto Rehoboam, saying, Thy father made our yoke grievous: now therefore make thou the grievous service of thy father, and his heavy yoke which he put upon us, lighter, and we will serve thee. And he said unto them, Depart yet for three days, then come again to me. And the people departed. And king Rehoboam consulted with the old men, that stood before Solomon his father while he yet lived, and said, How do ye advise that I may answer this people? And they spake unto him, saying, If thou wilt be a servant unto this people this day, and wilt serve them, and answer them, and speak good words to them, then they will be thy servants for ever. But he forsook the counsel of the old men, which they had given him, and consulted with the young men that were grown up with him, and which stood before him."*

Read the rest of the story. Rehoboam forsook godly counsel and chose instead to follow the ungodly advice of his peers—the young men—his "friends." It was literally the mistake of his life. It was all down hill from there. In 2 Chronicles 12:14, God sums up Rehoboam's life with these words, *"And he did evil, because he prepared not his heart to seek the LORD."* From early in his life, his decision to listen to ungodly counsel took him down a path of no return. He knew what was right, but deliberately made a choice to ignore godly counsel. Your story will be no different if you make such a choice.

"But ye have set at nought all my counsel, and would none of my reproof."—Proverbs 1:25

Mark it down—godly counsel will only come from people who unselfishly want God's perfect will for your life. You won't find good godly counsel from those who do not know and walk with God. It's impossible.

III. Why do you need counsel?

You might wonder, "If God is leading me, why should I get advice about it." It's simply about three key principles.

A. The principle of confirmation

You're not looking to godly counsel to "divine" your future like a fortune teller, a guru, or a palm reader. In truth, even the godliest of counselors has no more access to God than you do. Looking to a counselor in this way is not only unbiblical—it's spiritually lazy because it causes you to avoid all of the personal seeking of God that you're commanded to do. This is the sort of blind follower-ship that cults and false religions teach.

You don't need a priest to stand between you and God and reveal His will to you. That's a form of Nicolaitanism, which means, "to conquer the laity," and God makes it clear in Revelation chapter 2 that He actually hates this. Revelation 2:6 says, *"But this thou hast, that thou hatest the deeds of the Nicolaitans, which I also hate."*

Over the years, I've had a few friends who were too lazy to seek God for themselves. Rather than put forth the personal spiritual effort, they chose to just "go with the flow" and do whatever their parents or pastor told them to do. That looks and sounds noble on the surface, but it's rotten at the roots. It's noble to follow authority, but it's negligent to "ride on someone else's coat-tails." It's negligent to forsake seeking God's purposes personally.

This lack of personal depth and commitment may initially lead a person to *appear* to be following the Lord, but ultimately this plan will unravel from within as the

Devil wreaks havoc on this ungrounded individual. This person will not be like a *"tree planted by the rivers of water"* (Psalm 1). Rather, he will be easily uprooted and blown away.

So, you must not put your life in "auto-pilot" to blindly and indiscriminately be led around by the voices of others. These kinds of decisions never last.

Yet, you *do* need godly people, God-given authority, who want God's best for you. You need their guidance and advice, and you need their sound insight into the paths you are praying about. You need the collective wisdom of parents, pastors, and other spiritual leaders to confirm God's leading in your heart and to provide insight on how to best follow that leading.

And on those occasions when you come to a point that you simply don't know what God wants you to do, you need to be able to fall back on their authority in your life, which leads us to the second principle.

B. The principle of God-ordained authority

In your life, God has given you key authorities who love you, pray for you, know you, and perhaps understand you better than yourself! In the case of your parents this is absolutely true. If you have faithful Christian parents, they know you better than you know yourself at this point. God has given these authorities the wisdom they need to guide you. The Bible also calls this "understanding" or "perception."

Your parents have an amazing God-given perception that you must trust and listen to. Your pastor will also have a godly perception as well as a vast wealth of biblical knowledge and personal insight gained over years of dealing with crisis counseling and ministry situations. God has placed these divine authorities in your life on purpose. They are to be heard and followed (obeyed). Hebrews 13 teaches us to honor and obey them that have the rule over us. Ephesians 6 teaches us to obey and honor our parents.

At this point you might argue that you are a legal adult, but that's irrelevant. God has placed all of us under some sort of authority, and He expects us to obey and honor the biblical authorities in our lives regardless of our age. One of the biggest mistakes I see young adults make is that they think they have the legal right to stop listening to their parents when they turn eighteen. You may have the legal right, but that doesn't mean it's a smart thing to do! This is when you need their counsel and guidance the most!

God designed authority to be a hedge of protection in our lives to protect us from the fiery darts of Satan. Check this out. In Job 1:10, the Devil is talking to God about his inability to get to Job. He wants to hurt Job, but he is literally admitting to God that he can't get to him. Job is too safely protected within a "hedge." Look at it, *"Hast not thou made an hedge about him, and about his house, and about all that he hath on every side? thou hast blessed the work of his hands, and his substance is increased in the land."*

God-given authority in your life is just like that hedge in Job's life. So long as you stay in the hedge, you are protected from the attempts of Satan to ruin you. But beware, the moment you break out of that hedge, you are target practice for the Devil! Ecclesiastes 10:8 says it this way, *"He that diggeth a pit shall fall into it; and whoso breaketh an hedge, a serpent shall bite him."* You should be mature enough to voluntarily place yourself within the safe hedge of authority and to stay there by choice!

Authority is something that most young adults in our culture are trying to escape. It's not cool to be eighteen and to be under "authority." After all, you're free now! Rebellion is rampant!

I'm sorry to be the one to break it to you, but rebellion causes people to do stupid things! The sooner you get over your need to prove your independence, the sooner you will be able to avoid some serious mistakes. Being under authority is not about being treated like a "kid," it's about being a responsible adult.

I've often had young adults tell me "I don't just want to do what everybody thinks I should do." While I understand their reasoning, it's a mistake to have some inner aversion to following godly advice. That's nothing more than pride. If your heart is sincerely seeking God, you'll have no problem following the advice of godly people. I've seen some young adults do some amazingly ridiculous things out of sheer rebellion against authority and live to regret it. Authority is God's gift to you...so embrace it.

C. The principle of self-deception

We've already studied that you can deceive your own heart, and godly counsel is the last line of defense to sift through all of your heart's emotions and verify that you truly are yielding to God's best.

Think of it this way. God's Holy Spirit is not divided. If you are truly seeking and surrendered and if your counselors are truly godly and Spirit-filled, then you will all reach the same God-led conclusions about your decisions and your future. The same Holy

Spirit that leads you to one conclusion would not lead a multitude of other godly counselors to different conclusions. That's why this step is called the "safety net!" It's God's way of protecting you from yourself.

In other words, if you come to a conclusion that you feel is right for your future, and multiple godly counselors feel differently—you have to draw one of two conclusions. Either you are wrong and deceived… OR…your counselors are wrong and deceived. At this point, a choice is made to either trust yourself against counsel or trust godly counsel against yourself. Confused? Good…stay with me.

In summary, God expects you to seek counsel because:

1. He will use godly counselors to confirm His guidance.
2. He has ordained godly authority for your own protection.
3. He knows you can easily deceive yourself.

IV. How do you get godly counsel?

There is a right way and a wrong way to seeking godly counsel, and it's very easy to miss the boat on this.

A. *Refuse to fake getting counsel*

I've known of many occasions where an individual determined to take a course in life, and much like feigning prayer, they chose to "feign" getting counsel. It goes something like this.

Start with a desire. Perhaps I want to get married or start a career or purchase a coveted possession. Perhaps I just want to get out of the house and on my own. Soon this desire is so strong and my craving is so consuming that I make up my mind to do something about it. I make a wrong decision, even though I'm convinced that it's right.

After feigning prayer so I can make myself feel better, I decide to feign counsel to further salve my conscience. So, I set an appointment with a spiritual leader or determine a time to talk to Mom and Dad about my course. At the appointed time, I sit down, take a deep breath, and tell my "counselor" what I intend to do. At the end of my discourse I wrap up with "I've prayed about this, and I feel it's God's will." (Every time I say it, it makes me feel better—eventually I even start believing it.) Finally, I say something like "So, what's your opinion?" At this point I feel really good about myself. After all, I'm obeying the Word of God in seeking godly counsel, right? Wrong.

Actually, all I've done is backed my potential counselor into a corner and forced them with one of two difficult options. Support me in this and watch me mess up my life…or try to oppose me and get ready for World War III! I haven't asked for guidance, advice, or insight. I haven't come with a seeking or surrendered heart. I'm not prepared to hear *any* answer, especially an honest one, and I'm ready to move on with my decision regardless of what anyone thinks. This is not what getting godly counsel is about—at all!

B. Refuse to force your counselors to support you
What parent or pastor in their right mind is going to stand in strong opposition against a mind so firmly made up? They may initially try to talk some sense

into you, but eventually they will choose the "support" avenue and simply hope for the best. In other words, if you choose to marry a person your parents do not approve of, they may try to resist at first, but eventually they will do what all good parents will do—support you and hope it works out somehow. It never does.

I'm saying this, it's very easy to convince yourself that you are getting counsel when really all you are doing is insisting on approval for a decision you've already made. It's easy to corner your authorities into supporting your decision whether they like it or not. What other options do they have—disown you? Never see the grandkids at Christmas? Start a relationship with their future in-laws with war paint on? I don't think so. Forcing your counselors to "grin and bear it" is not what the Bible teaches you to do.

Sincerely getting godly counsel is the exact opposite of what I've just described, and it is one of God's quickest ways to verify your true heart and direction.

So, now that you know how "not" to get counsel, here's what you should do:

C. Have a multitude of godly counselors
The Bible principle in this is very clear.

*"Where no counsel is, the people fall: but in the **multitude of counsellors** there is safety."*—Proverbs 11:14

"Without counsel purposes are disappointed: but in the multitude of counsellors they are established."
—Proverbs 15:22

God wants you to have a number of godly people that you will turn to for advice, and at the top of the list should be your parents and your pastor.

In addition to this list you could add godly teachers, assistant pastors, grandparents, deacons, etc. Just take a minute and look at the landscape of godly leadership in your life. God has probably given you a good number of godly people who would be more than happy to give you biblical advice. So, go to them. Set up appointments, make phone calls, get as many people on your team of godly counselors as you can. You're going to need all the insight you can get.

Most importantly, make sure that your counselors are truly godly people. I don't mean perfect, just faithful in walking with God and seeking Him. You are about to entrust your future to these people, so choose people with a proven track record of faithfulness. Choose counselors who will approach giving you advice with fear and trembling. This needs to be someone who will literally be absolutely terrified of counseling you with anything but biblical, Christ-centered advice.

D. Listen with an open heart

"The way of a fool is right in his own eyes: but he that hearkeneth unto counsel is wise."—Proverbs 12:15

*"Hear **counsel**, and receive instruction, that thou mayest be wise in thy latter end."*—Proverbs 19:20

When you step into a counseling appointment, don't have your mind made up. That's a terrible mistake, not to mention a waste of time. Have an open heart and a willing spirit. Don't sit down and start to "sell" your point of view. Don't even present your point of view.

Just lay out the options, explain your search for God's will, and then ask for honest insight and advice.

In that moment of counsel, what you need the most is to know the impressions of the Holy Spirit on this person's heart in regard to your situation. You want to hear the Scriptures that this person brings to the table. You want this godly counselor to speak freely and openly about what the Lord is guiding him to say. You want him to be totally and completely honest, and you want to be ready to hear and receive *any* answer—not just the ones you want to hear. Your counselor needs to be willing to even hurt your feelings if that's what it takes to be truthful and transparent. And you should want the truth so badly, that you're willing to take it.

Ask for honesty. Alleviate his fears that you might not want the full truth. Ask for this person to be brutally transparent if they sense any danger, deception, or error in your circumstances.

Finally, ask this person this question, "If the decision were yours to make for me, what do you really believe is God's will in this?" The Bible principle for this is stated this way, *"Counsel in the heart of man is like deep water; but a man of understanding will draw it out"* (Proverbs 20:5). Work at drawing out the real scriptural opinions and admonitions of your counselors.

E. Look for either confirmation or contradiction to your decision

At this point, when your counselor speaks, one of two things will happen. Either the counsel will confirm God's leading in your heart or it will contradict it. As you talk to a multitude of counselors, this same thing will happen over and over—either **confirmation** or **contradiction**.

Here's the best part! If you have truly surrendered to God, and if you have honestly sought the advice of godly people, your multitude of counsel will fall directly in line with the internal voice of God (which your counselors may or may not know about).

Do you get it? God will use the voices of a multitude of counselors to independently confirm what He placed on your heart in the first place. This forms a closed case for a right decision. At this point, you can have the final full peace that you are making a right choice, *and* you have the full authority of Scriptures and the full support of God's promises backing you up. You're now in good hands with God's Word, God's truth, and God's promise for a bright future!

Godly counsel—what a wonderful gift from God! Next to wisdom, it's probably the most untapped resource in the Christian life. Imagine the wealth of knowledge and insight that young adults all over the world turn away from every day!

F. Avoid a "counsel debate"

Along these lines, be careful about "shopping counsel" or "comparing counsel" to try to find what you want to hear. The principle of hearing a multitude of godly counselors is that the same Holy Spirit will impress the same leading on all of their hearts. In addition to this, different counselors will give you different insights and varying vantage points that will all prove helpful as you make your decision.

In the rare situation when the advice from two or more "godly counselors" comes into direct contradiction with each other be careful about casting judgment or forming a premature opinion. For example, you may have a spiritual leader who gives advice that contradicts your parent's advice. It could easily happen if that leader doesn't know what your parents have advised.

At this point you should hear the counsel, weigh it carefully, discuss it with your parents or other "authority," and fall back on the authority principle in knowing how to apply the counsel. In other words, depend on your closest authority to guide you through the questions. Whatever you do, don't pit one counselor against another. Don't withhold critical information that could put them in opposition, and don't negatively compare them against each other. (Eg: "Well, so and so said this...")

The point is, when talking to multiple people about the same issue, you must avoid getting into a "counsel debate." That will derail the whole process all together and potentially hurt some good people in your life.

V. Don't defy a multitude of godly counselors

In conclusion, mark this down. If you have determined a course of action that your godly counselors do not concur on...don't make a move. You cannot walk the tightrope outside of the safety net and hope to survive. There is something terribly wrong with this picture. Somewhere along the path you got off course—guaranteed. If you can talk to godly person after godly person who feels that you are making a wrong decision—you are! Just ask yourself this, "If the Holy Spirit is confirming this in me, why isn't He confirming this in others?"

By the way, it may not mean that you're totally "off your rocker." It may just mean that God wants you to wait for His timing.

Don't be afraid of getting godly advice. Be afraid not to! Don't be so arrogant as to think that you can walk the tightrope of life without ever making a wrong decision. Get counsel! Your circumstances are not new! There are many people who have stood where you stand and felt what you feel! So, go get their advice and follow it. You'll save yourself a lot of heartache!

String that safety net across your path, tie it down tightly, and then don't be afraid to fall into it and find out that you were about to make a wrong decision. In fact, be like a trapeze artist—get real comfortable with falling into the safety net. There's nothing to fear about it!

When godly counsel contradicts the intents of your heart, walk softly stranger! You're on very thin ice and you need to re-think, re-pray, and re-search this whole process.

Psalm 33:11 says, *"The counsel of the LORD standeth for ever, the thoughts of his heart to all generations."* Proverbs 21:30 says, *"There is no wisdom nor understanding nor counsel against the LORD."*

"Hear counsel, and receive instruction, that thou mayest be wise in thy latter end."—Proverbs 19:20

Discussion Questions

1. How do you verify God's leading in a decision?
2. List the two types of counsel.
3. Why is getting counsel important?
4. If your counselors are not in agreement regarding a decision, what should you do?
5. If God gives you a direction, why is it so critical that you seek counsel before you make a final decision?
6. List several names of "godly counselors" you can go to when making a decision, and explain why you can trust them.
7. How and why do people fake getting counsel?
8. Describe a time in your life when you made a decision without or against godly counsel and explain why you regret it.

Memory Verse

"The way of a fool is right in his own eyes: but he that hearkeneth unto counsel is wise."—Proverbs 12:15

Lesson Notes

_____

_____

_____

_____

_____

_____

_____

_____

_____

_____

_____

_____

_____

_____

_____

_____

_____

_____

_____

_____

_____

_____

_____

_____

_____

_____

_____

_____

_____

Lesson Notes

Don't Just Stand There; Set That Ship On Fire!

The Testing of a Well-Made Decision

Text

"But none of these things move me, neither count I my life dear unto myself, so that I might finish my course with joy, and the ministry, which I have received of the Lord Jesus, to testify the gospel of the grace of God."—Acts 20:24

"But he knoweth the way that I take: when he hath tried me, I shall come forth as gold."—Job 23:10

Lesson Aim

The lesson teaches that every decision is immediately tested with opposition from the enemy. Every good decision will be opposed, and your students should expect the tests and prepare to face them in God's strength.

Teaching Outline

I. Move it or lose it; it's time for action!
   A. Determine to move forward.
   B. Expect the Devil to distract, detour, or delay you. (Acts 20:24)
   C. Express faith and make your decision.

II. Expect immediate testing of a decision.
   A. Every right decision is followed by immediate testing. (2 Corinthians 4:16–17)

B. The testing of your decision will lead to greater blessings.

III. What kind of "promised land" is this?
    A. God's blessings are more than you can handle.
    B. God is preparing you to be strong enough for His future blessings.

IV. There are three critical areas of testing.
    A. You are tested your first year or two of college.
    B. You are tested your first few years of marriage.
    C. You are tested your first few years of faithfulness to God.

V. How do you pass the testing of your decision?
    A. Refuse to entertain doubts.
    B. Renew your commitment to God's call.
    C. Return to Scripture. (Isaiah 40:31)
    D. Remember God's promises. (Romans 8:37; 1 Corinthians 15:58; 2 Corinthians 4:1, 8–9; 2 Corinthians 12:10; 2 Timothy 1:12; Hebrews 12:1–3; James 1:2–4; 1 Corinthians 16:13)
    E. Renew your strength in God.

fifteen

Don't Just Stand There; Set That Ship On Fire!

The Testing of a Well-Made Decision

At this point, you should very clearly understand what God has led you to do, and you should be ready to finalize your decision. If you have truly followed the principles of God's Word, you will not only have clarity of heart, but you will also have the support of godly authorities in your life and the promises of Scripture as the foundation of your decision. In addition to this, you should have deep purpose and commitment to the path that God has led you down.

I. Move it or lose it; it's time for action!

Now you have a choice. Either follow God or retreat. It's quite simple really. You've come to the "precipice" of action, and now it's time to "leap!" It's literally time to take a deep breath and step forward in faith without wavering.

It doesn't matter if you *want* to do what God has led you to do. Your emotions will catch up later, and God will work all that out. It doesn't matter if you can't see *how* it's all going to work out—that's the faith part. It doesn't even matter if it makes sense. The point is you have sought the Lord, and He has led you and confirmed His leading—so it's time to do it! It's time to muster up the courageous spirit that Joshua had and step out across the Jordan River!

It's at this point that many young adults come so close to following God, and then suddenly for some unforeseen reason, they chicken out. They get so close to tasting the reality of their faith, and like a scared animal, they turn and run. DON'T DO THIS!

Rather, determine that you will proceed forward. Determine that you will not retreat or run. With a fierce commitment and fiery certainty, choose to commit wholeheartedly to God's leading in your life. Say with the Apostle Paul, *"But none of these things move me, neither count I my life dear unto myself, so that I might finish my course with joy, and the ministry, which I have received of the Lord Jesus, to testify the gospel of the grace of God"* (Acts 20:24).

There is a season of time between *God's* confirmation and *your* action when the Devil will do everything within his power to "spook" you out of following God. This is when he will work overtime to deceive, distract, and detour your future.

In addition to this, he will bring to your mind every negative thought you could ever have about the possibilities of God's will. He will remind you of all the things you "don't want to do." He will be ruthless and relentless, raising questions and doubts and doing everything he can to cheat you out of the greatest happiness you could imagine!

Don't fall for it! Stay the course. Commit to God's will and follow Him with unyielding passion. Determine that God's leading will not come into question, and quickly turn your decision into action. Immediately begin doing what God has told you. Obey right away and leave no time for reconsideration. Reconsidering would simply give place to defiance against God, and defiance is not an option.

Honestly, in spite of the spiritual opposition you might sense, my guess is that you will be pretty eager to go forward at this point. After all this time of seeking and praying, you finally know God's will—at least for the immediate future. What a relief! Now, rather than anticipating your future, you can begin fulfilling it!

II. Expect immediate testing of a decision

Friend, it's time for you to go ashore in God's will for your life…but before you do, you need to set fire to the ship! You need to determine there is no retreat in the will of God. There is no reconsidering the direct leading of God in your life. You must obey with absolute abandon, leaving yourself no room for withdrawal. Paul said it this way in Romans 11:29, *"For the gifts and calling of God are without repentance."* In other words—there's no turning back!

There's a reason that this commitment is so needful at this point. You are about to enter into a critical proving time for your decision and for your future. I call it "the testing of the decision." It's not the testing of God's leading. (That's already been taken care of.) The testing of the decision involves the proving of your commitment and resolve in the decision. In other words—just how committed are you to seeing this decision through to fruition? Before you will enjoy the mountain top experiences of God's will, you'll have to climb the mountain of testing.

You see, the Devil will not only work against you before you finalize your decision, he will also fight you shortly after you've made your decision. Here's what I mean.

Almost every major decision of your life will be followed by an immediate time of testing that either solidifies or uproots the decision. The strategy is that the Devil will try to question your direction and reverse your decision before you've had time to really settle in and begin to experience the long term fruit of doing right!

Don't expect your world to be perfect and your path to be effortless the moment you decide to follow God. In fact, you should expect the exact opposite. You should expect spiritual opposition (Ephesians 6:12) and even emotional upheaval. (Wow, following God sounds exciting, doesn't it?) You should expect trials—intended by God to strengthen and settle you, but intended by Satan to discourage and frustrate you. Again, Paul referred to this testing in 2 Corinthians 4:16–17, *"For which cause we faint not; but though our outward man perish, yet the inward man is renewed day by day. For our light affliction, which is but for a moment, worketh for us a far more exceeding and eternal weight of glory."*

Throughout your spiritual journey, you will face spiritual opposition, but perhaps never as intense as during this time, and perhaps never at such a critical moment as this. The moment you set out to obey God, you will enter into a proving time that tests you, prepares you, and paves the way for future blessings.

It's as though your decision is a seedling tree that will one day become a mighty oak—solid and unmovable. Yet, while it is young and fragile, the Devil wants to step on it, crush it, and destroy it. It will take the forces of the elements and a lot of time for your decision to become rooted deep, and there will be many times along the journey that you will want to look back and question the validity of your decision, but don't!

Sadly, the spiritual landscape is littered with casualties from this "crisis point." Many people follow God, only to be scared back into the ship of retreat because of unexpected battles or trials. Many Christians hear God's voice and obey Him only to turn and run for the hills at the first sign of spiritual opposition. No, the "promised land" of God's will is not intended for the weak or faint-hearted. It is intended for those who are fully committed to pressing forward with the ships burning behind them.

Now, I don't want to scare you. When you choose to obey God you are certainly in store for happiness, blessings, and awesome joy—but first you're going to have to pass some tests. You're going to come to your own "crisis point" where you will be tempted to entertain doubts and questions. You should expect this, and you should determine to silence the doubts immediately.

Your "major" decisions in life may take years to mature and come to full fruition, but don't let that discourage you…it's going to be well worth the journey!

III. What kind of "promised land" is this?

Remember our lesson about courage and our talk about Joshua? Well, Joshua *was* courageous, and he *did* follow God across that Jordan River, but what he found on the other side was certainly no "promised land." "War-land" or "Battle-land" would have been a more appropriate name.

His decision to be courageous and follow God led the children of Israel into a series of spiritual tests and physical battles unlike any they had ever faced. They had never been so close to the fulfillment of God's promises and never so tested either!

City after city, battle after battle, Joshua repeatedly followed God and did exactly as he was told. He was clinging to God's promise that this land of battles would one day be conquered, and a "promised land" could be claimed.

Before the nation of Israel could ever enjoy the "milk and honey" of the Promised Land, they had to deal with the "blood and guts" of the battlefield. Even so, as you follow God into a faith-based decision, you can be sure you will fight some spiritual battles before you experience the real blessings of such obedience.

Right about now, you might be asking, "Why would God answer my obedience with such testing?" I'm glad you asked. There are several reasons.

A. God's blessings are more than you can handle

Though you've surrendered, you're nowhere near being prepared to properly handle all that He plans to give you. His goodness will be so abundant and His blessings so awesome, that He's going to have to strengthen you and prepare you for them. Every battle and every testing will take you one step closer to being able to properly enjoy the blessings God has in store.

B. God is preparing you to be strong enough for His future blessings

Without the testing of your decision, you'll never experience the blessings! No pain, no gain.

As a side note, it's not all bad. I don't want you to get the idea that as soon as you follow God, life gets miserable and difficult. It's not like that at all. You simply get "put to the test." Before you can really savor the blessings, your resolve and commitment are going to be tested and tried. Your decision will endure a spiritual "refining" process that will solidify it deep within.

Every Bible college student must face the despair of homesickness before they can gain the benefits of ministry training. Every marriage must withstand the test of relational disagreements before a stronger love can be forged. Every ministry intern must withstand the tests of personal sacrifice before real fruit can be seen.

So, expect the testing of your decision. Expect doubts to come and hesitation to invade your heart. Expect discouragement and frustration from time to time. Expect to lose some sleep dealing with issues of spiritual growth. Know that the Devil will try to get you to turn back, but know that God will use these tests to prepare you for awesome blessings!

IV. There are three critical areas of testing

For every young adult, there are three primary periods of life when the Devil will really test your decisions.

A. You are tested your first year or two of college

When you choose to follow God to the right college, you can be sure that the first year will be a proving time. You will face many opportunities to retreat, rethink your decision, and renege on your surrender to the Lord.

B. You are tested your first few years of marriage

As wonderful as those first few years are, they also include many times of intense "life-shaping" as two become one. Any time you blend two individual lives into one, you're going to experience some testing. Most people enter into a marriage completely ignorant of the storms that they will sail through together. Then, rather than face the storms together, they jump ship. They forget that when the storm is over, sunny skies return and sailing skills are stronger.

C. You are tested your first few years of faithfulness to God

This may be in reference to your faithfulness to God as a layperson in your local church, or it may be your faithfulness in full-time ministry. Whether in ministry or secular work, you can be sure that your faithfulness to the Lord will be tested when you are "on your own."

In my life, these three periods were critical times of testing. That's not to say that there weren't blessings during these times, and it's not to say that I won't still experience future tests in my life. It's just that these periods seemed to be more intense. It's as though the Devil was deliberately trying to destroy my direction early in the journey.

Stand guard over your heart during these seasons when your decisions are still "fresh" or "new." Once the "cement dries," once you survive a few storms—you won't be as easily moved.

V. How do you pass the testing of your decision?

How do you pass these decision tests so that you can really see the long-term fruit of your decision? Here are a few suggestions.

A. Refuse to entertain doubts

If God led you, then don't ever let anything bring that leading into question! You may have heard the saying "Don't doubt in the night what God gave you in the light." Simply refuse to entertain any thought that you made a wrong decision. I really believe the Devil gives these initial thoughts as "bait." If you don't "bite," you won't get reeled in!

B. Renew your commitment to God's call

When tests come, simply renew your commitment to Christ and to following what you know to be right. Strengthen your stand and deepen your roots. Stand strong in what you know is right, and your storm will eventually subside, leaving you stronger and more prepared.

C. Return to Scripture

God's Word will renew your strength, settle your doubts, and help you to mount up with wings. (Isaiah 40:31) Rather than doubting your direction, go to the Word of God and seek His power.

D. Remember God's promises

God has given you hundreds of awesome promises to sustain you through times of testing and proving. Here are just a few that might help to strengthen you during the testing of your decision.

"Nay, in all these things we are more than conquerors through him that loved us."—Romans 8:37

"Therefore, my beloved brethren, be ye stedfast, unmoveable, always abounding in the work of the Lord, forasmuch as ye know that your labour is not in vain in the Lord."—1 Corinthians 15:58

"Therefore seeing we have this ministry, as we have received mercy, we faint not;"—2 Corinthians 4:1

"We are troubled on every side, yet not distressed; we are perplexed, but not in despair; Persecuted, but not forsaken; cast down, but not destroyed;"
—2 Corinthians 4:8–9

"Therefore I take pleasure in infirmities, in reproaches, in necessities, in persecutions, in distresses for Christ's sake: for when I am weak, then am I strong."
—2 Corinthians 12:10

"For the which cause I also suffer these things: nevertheless I am not ashamed: for I know whom I have believed, and am persuaded that he is able to keep that which I have committed unto him against that day."
—2 Timothy 1:12

"Wherefore seeing we also are compassed about with so great a cloud of witnesses, let us lay aside every weight, and the sin which doth so easily beset us, and let us run with patience the race that is set before us, Looking unto Jesus the author and finisher of our faith; who for the joy that was set before him endured the cross, despising the

shame, and is set down at the right hand of the throne of God. For consider him that endured such contradiction of sinners against himself, lest ye be wearied and faint in your minds."—Hebrews 12:1–3

"*My brethren, count it all joy when ye fall into divers temptations; Knowing this, that the trying of your faith worketh patience. But let patience have her perfect work, that ye may be perfect and entire, wanting nothing.*" —James 1:2–4

"*Watch ye, stand fast in the faith, quit you like men, be strong.*"—1 Corinthians 16:13

Anything that moves forward will face adversity and friction. Adversity in your spiritual life proves that you are moving forward, and also puts the power of God into motion in your life. He will sustain you, strengthen you, comfort you, and renew you. Just like He promised Joshua—He will be with you through every battle!

E. *Renew your strength in God*

This is serious stuff. If you're not careful, you'll seek the Lord carefully for your future only to be disappointed by the tests you face when you get there.

Take hope…the testing is worth it. For every test that God leads you through, there is an equal or greater reward. For every storm your marriage endures, there is a stronger love to be gained. For every ministry obstacle you overcome, there is a greater fruit to be harvested. For every personal doubt you settle, there is a personal reward to be treasured—in the perfect will of God. For every year you stay faithful to God, there is a truckload of blessings and fruit that you will enjoy somewhere down the line.

So, get moving. If God has brought you to the point of confirmation, then it's time to leap! Go for it! His promises will sustain you through every test, and His grace will sustain you through every doubt. The testing of your decision will simply be a pathway of preparation for God's greatest plans.

"But he knoweth the way that I take: when he hath tried me, I shall come forth as gold."—Job 23:10

Discussion Questions

1. What is every right decision followed by?
2. By testing your decision, what is God preparing you for?
3. List the three critical areas of testing.
4. What are the five steps to passing the testing of your decision?
5. What could happen if you don't intentionally determine to move forward in your decision?
6. What are God's promises to you during the testing of your decision?
7. Why do you think your decisions for college and marriage are so vigorously tested during the beginning years?
8. How can you fail the testing of your decision? What habits could you start developing this week to keep this from happening?

Memory Verse

"Therefore I take pleasure in infirmities, in reproaches, in necessities, in persecutions, in distresses for Christ's sake: for when I am weak, then am I strong."—2 Corinthians 12:10

Lesson Notes

What Do You Do With a Pet Chicken?

Returning to God's Will from Bad Decisions

Text

And when they were at Salamis, they preached the word of God in the synagogues of the Jews: and they had also John to their minister."—Acts 13:5

And some days after Paul said unto Barnabas, Let us go again and visit our brethren in every city where we have preached the word of the LORD, and see how they do. And Barnabas determined to take with them John, whose surname was Mark. But Paul thought not good to take him with them, who departed from them from Pamphylia, and went not with them to the work. And the contention was so sharp between them, that they departed asunder one from the other: and so Barnabas took Mark, and sailed unto Cyprus;"—Acts 15:36–39

"Only Luke is with me. Take Mark, and bring him with thee: for he is profitable to me for the ministry."—2 Timothy 4:11

"Brethren, I count not myself to have apprehended: but this one thing I do, forgetting those things which are behind, and reaching forth unto those things which are before, I press toward the mark for the prize of the high calling of God in Christ Jesus."—Philippians 3:13–14

"And we know that all things work together for good to them that love God, to them who are the called according to his purpose."—Romans 8:28

Lesson Aim

This lesson is designed to help students understand God's grace and mercy when it comes to repenting of bad decisions and undergoing a process of restoration. The lesson is designed to encourage students not to give up when they've made a bad decision, but rather to respond properly to God's leading and to get back on the right track.

Teaching Outline

I. A second chance in God's will (Acts 15:36–39)

    A. John Mark started serving God faithfully.

    B. John Mark forsook God's work.

    C. John Mark returned to God and became effective in the ministry. (2 Timothy 4:11)

II. Starting God's perfect will today

    A. What is behind you cannot be changed.

    B. God has forgotten what is behind you. (Philippians 3:13–14)

    C. God has future blessings if you will follow Him today.

    D. Determine to live God's will from today forward.

III. Lingering damage from the "Mistake Zone"

    A. Every bad decision has bad consequences.

    B. Even bad consequences can be worked together for good. (Romans 8:26–28)

IV. A window of reversal (Romans 2:4)

    A. Many bad decisions cannot be undone.

    B. Many bad decisions can be undone.

    C. Don't be too proud to undo a bad decision before it is too late.

sixteen

What Do You Do With a Pet Chicken?

Returning to God's Will from Bad Decisions

I made a really, really bad decision when I was in fifth grade. I had a pet chicken. I thought it would be cool. I thought all the kids would like me. I thought I could start a new fad in my state—domesticated chickens. I pictured taming my chicken, putting him on a leash, taking him for walks, teaching him tricks. I didn't even know that chickens aren't 'hims' at all…they're "hers!" It was a sad day when I realized I had named my *female* chicken with a *boy's* name. To make a bad situation worse, with three boys in the home, we soon had three chickens!

In the process of getting my chicken, no one told me that chickens are about 90% poop. I hate to be crude, but that's just the fact. It only took about a week for our yard to look like a "white Christmas" on a frosty December morning. Seemingly over night, that place went from being green grass to being the chicken-dung *capital* of the world! Even the rectangular fence was "white-capped"! It's no wonder we began to lose interest in playing in the pen! Suddenly our "beloved" pet chickens seemed more like clucking caulking guns!

With all of that, came a smell unlike any cow pasture I've ever smelled. It was unbelievable. Just being in the mere vicinity of our backyard became an unpleasant nasal experience.

In a matter of a few days these chickens went from being the most loved and well cared for chickens on the planet to being the most neglected, renegade fowls imaginable. Our backyard pen became a sort of "chicken slum" for unwanted and abandoned chickens. We hated even the thought of throwing feed into that pen! It seemed like such a waste of good feed! Emphasis on "waste!"

I'll never forget the moment my mom suggested that we get rid of the chickens. I'm sure she thought she was going to break our hearts, but we were only too willing to reclaim our backyard for childhood play. It took all of two seconds to talk us into giving them up to some hungry families who lived in the vicinity of our country property. In a few short days we were able to hose down our "winter wonderland" and reclaim our childhood territory; while at the same time, some hungry stomachs were filled with our sumptuous pets! It was a win-win situation!

I learned a valuable lesson through that experience. Simply put, chickens are not pets…they're food. Chickens were not designed to be domesticated; they were designed to be battered and fried. They were not made to tame and train; they were made to dip and devour. My personal preference is barbecue sauce. Chickens were not given to be guided…they were given to be grilled!

Chickens cannot be domesticated, and when some poor soul tries, he's going to end up with more "poop" than he can deal with. It's a fact of life. It's a law of nature. When you try to domesticate chickens you upset the delicate balance of the "circle of life" and the whole "ecosystem" gets out of whack.

The main lesson I learned from my pet chicken incident is that poop doesn't have to be permanent! Deciding to *have* pet chickens didn't mean we had to *keep* pet chickens. It's too bad it took my mom's prompting to help us learn that lesson, or we would have been rid of those chickens a lot sooner. The fact is I had to deal with that "white Christmas" for about three weeks longer than I wanted to because I was too afraid to tell my mom that we had made a grave, grave mistake!

So, what are you going to do with your mistakes…your bad decisions? Perhaps you've already made some. Perhaps you're standing up to your neck in "bad decisions," and you're not sure what to do. Well, hopefully you can learn the same lesson I did. Let's talk about it…

Rahab the harlot, David the adulterer, Peter the denier, Jonah the runner, Moses the murderer, Mark the deserter, Paul the persecutor—do these names ring any bells with you? They are Bible characters that all made some tragic decisions at one time or another.

If you had known them during their time of "bad choices," you wouldn't have given them much hope. You wouldn't have wanted to be their best friend, and you wouldn't have voted them the "most likely to succeed."

Yet, somewhere, somehow in all of their lives, they were given a second chance. In the midst of their bad choices, God touched their lives and redirected their futures by His grace. You probably know most of the stories, and in fact I'm sure there are many more in Scripture, but I want you to look closely at one in particular.

I. A second chance in God's will

John Mark was a young man who was serving the Lord under the ministry of the Apostle Paul. You could call him an "intern." Acts 13:5 says that he was serving with Paul and Barnabas as their minister. Apparently he made a decision to follow God into the ministry. Later, the book of Acts tells us that John Mark had left the ministry at some point. Here's the story:

> "And some days after Paul said unto Barnabas, Let us go again and visit our brethren in every city where we have preached the word of the Lord, and see how they do. And Barnabas determined to take with them John, whose surname was Mark. But Paul thought not good to take him with them, who departed from them from Pamphylia, and went not with them to the work. And the contention was so sharp between them, that they departed asunder one from the other: and so Barnabas took Mark, and sailed unto Cyprus;"—Acts 15:36–39

For whatever reason, John Mark apparently deserted the work and later wanted to re-enter the ministry. He made a bad decision and wanted to return to the perfect will of God for his life. Paul refused him, but Barnabas took him back. This caused a division between Barnabas and Paul that caused them to part ways.

Here's the rest of the story. Fast forward to the end of the Apostle Paul's life and look at what he says about John Mark. The Bible says in 2 Timothy 4:11, *"Only Luke is with me. Take Mark, and bring him with thee: for he is profitable to me for the ministry."*

God not only restored John Mark to the ministry, but he apparently used him in a unique and effective way. John Mark did indeed have a second chance, and so do you if you've already made some bad decisions.

II. Starting God's perfect will today

Perhaps you can look back at mistakes you've already made in the "Mistake Zone." Perhaps you've already passed through many of the major decisions we've talked about, and you're wondering exactly where you are on the "road map" of God's will. Maybe you feel like you're not even on the map anymore.

That could potentially be a depressing and discouraging feeling in light of all the principles that we've studied. Please don't allow yourself to feel that despair. Rather than revisit "what might have been," let's take the advice of one of the Bible's biggest "come-back-kids"—the Apostle Paul.

Here is a man who literally tried to destroy the church of Jesus Christ. He was a persecutor and a murderer. The new Christians of the first century were terrified of him! Yet, God reached out of Heaven, saved him, and gave him a new mission in life.

Can you imagine the guilt, the discouragement, the despair that the Apostle Paul could have constantly lived with? Can you imagine how the Devil must have constantly dredged up the past, reminding him of the Christians he had killed or persecuted? This could have potentially had a crippling effect—a paralyzing impact—on the future ministry of Paul! Think about that!

Had Paul continued to dwell on his past decisions, he could have literally missed all that God had in store for the future! Here's what he said about his past, *"Brethren, I count not myself to have apprehended: but this one thing I do, forgetting those things which are behind, and reaching forth unto those things which are before, I press toward the mark for the prize of the high calling of God in Christ Jesus"* (Philippians 3:13–14).

There is a beautiful principle about God's will in this passage. God's perfect will for your future always starts today! In other words, what's behind you cannot be changed, but what's ahead of you most certainly can be! Wherever you are in the journey of life, there is never a time when God doesn't have a perfect will for you from this day forward. There's no use crying over spilt milk! There's no sense in throwing away His blessings in the future because of bad decisions in the past. Thanks to God's awesome plan, we can literally put the past behind us and anticipate a bright future in His will.

God has a way of dealing with your bad decisions. It's called the Cross! He sent Jesus to die in your place on the Cross so that He could forgive and forget your past. And, if you have trusted Him as your Saviour, then He truly has forgotten your past! Have you? Of course not, and the Devil will continually try to use your past to keep you from surrendering your future! The sad part is many people fall for this deception.

Perhaps we could sit and talk about what God's will for your life "might have been" if only you hadn't (fill in the blank.) Perhaps you've been thinking these thoughts as you've read this book. So get this—there is nothing productive or spiritual about such thinking. It can only be destructive.

There is nothing about your sinful past that God remembers, and there is nothing about your future that He doesn't want to bless! That's how great His grace really is. That's how wonderful it is to belong to Him!

Your only choice in the face of this kind of "self-incrimination" is to either wallow in the past for the rest of your life or accept God's unconditional forgiveness and start living in His perfect will right now! Don't fall for the lie that you missed it. You haven't missed what is yet to come! If anything, let your bad decisions of the past be the catalyst that keeps you from "missing out" on anything else that God might have waiting for you! Let the lessons you learned yesterday be your turning point today.

Remember how we talked about God's eternal plan? Well, the fact that your heart is still beating is evidence that you still have a role to play in that plan! God hasn't left you on this earth for no reason! If you're breathing, then you still have a second chance—you too can be a "come-back-kid" in the story of God's unfolding purpose!

So, quit listening to the lies of your past and start surrendering to God's perfect will today. I don't care what you've done—it's still going to be awesome! The choice is yours, and your track record for "right decision-making" could start right now.

III. Lingering damage from the "Mistake Zone"

If you've made some bad decisions in the past, be aware that there may be some lifelong consequences that cannot be removed. That doesn't mean that God hasn't forgiven you or that He cannot use you. It simply means that bad decisions cannot be undone.

I could write for hours of the hundreds of "come-back" stories that I know of. These are amazing stories of people who made tragic decisions, experienced the tragic results, and then determined to be restored to God's purposes by His awesome grace! The pain and regrets of the past are a very real part of their lives, but the hope and blessings of their present lives in God's will are something they wouldn't have missed out on!

Yet, bad decisions often have bad consequences. When a young lady has a baby out of wedlock, that new life will bring a reminder of a past failure for many years to come. When a family experiences a divorce, there are multiple lingering effects of that separation. When someone experiences substance abuse, pre-marital sex, or a hedonistic lifestyle there are long-term consequences emotionally, mentally, and physically.

I bring this up not to "rub it in your face" but simply to say the presence of these lingering effects does not in any way negate the possibility of future blessings or usefulness to God. In fact, God's promise to you is directly opposed to that thinking.

Romans 8 shares an awesome passage about the purposes of God, and right in the middle of this passage, God says to you *"Likewise the Spirit also helpeth our infirmities: for we know not what we should pray for as we ought: but the Spirit itself maketh intercession for us with groanings which cannot be uttered. And he that searcheth the hearts knoweth what is the mind of the Spirit, because he maketh intercession for the saints according to the will of God. And we know that all things work together for good to them that love God, to them who are the called according to his purpose"* (Romans 8:26–28).

This passage promises that God is not only on your side, but He is literally planning to make *"all things work together for good."* In other words, He will somehow bring good results out of your bad decisions if you will surrender to His will. He will take your past, forgive it, and then turn it around for good in His eternal plan. What a promise!

It doesn't mean the effects are gone. It doesn't mean we can just sin willfully and claim Romans 8:28. It just means that God's grace and wisdom will somehow bring good from bad when we determine to love God and live according to His purposes.

This means that we are all "without excuse." Having a past of bad decisions doesn't excuse you from living in God's will right now. God's grace levels the playing field and gives everybody the same second chance for the future.

So beware of the battle scars of the "Mistake Zone." Perhaps you're coming toward the end of your own "Mistake Zone," and you didn't fare so well. The proper response would be to get on your knees before God, confess whatever sin is remaining, and then forget the things that are behind and start pressing forward. You may forever bear the scars and wounds of the "Mistake Zone," but that's no reason to keep from experiencing God's best from this day forward.

IV. A window of reversal

Before you put this lesson behind you, there's one more thing you need to know about bad decisions.

Sometimes—not all the time—but sometimes, a bad decision can be quickly reversed with relatively little damage being done to your life. This isn't the case with all major decisions, but it is with many of them. I would call it a 'window of reversal." It's really a wonderful evidence of God's amazing grace and patience with us, and you need to be aware of it.

It's almost like God leaves the window of decision open for a few moments after you've made a bad decision. It's like He's giving you a chance to jump back through the window and still do things His way. The length of time that this "window" is open often varies greatly from decision to decision. Usually the circumstances vary widely so it's somewhat unpredictable, but I've seen that window open many times in the lives of young adults.

Now, there are many decisions that cannot be undone. In these cases, the damage is done the moment your decision is final. There's no preventing the pain at this point. You are now a slave of the consequences whether you like it or not.

For instance, if you decide to have immoral relationships, you are risking your very life—a decision that cannot be undone with effects that cannot be reversed. If you get married, that decision cannot be reversed or retreated from. There are many such "leaps" that cannot be undone.

Yet, there are some decisions where the window stays open and the damage hasn't been done.

I know young adults who determined to go against God's will in their college decision. In this case, up until the class registration deadline, their decision is "reversible!" In other words, there's a "sliver" of time when they can choose to come back to God's will and follow His leading with minimal spiritual effects.

Sadly, most people never get back through the window. Most people are too far away from God in the process of a bad decision to even see the "window of reversal" much less to jump back through it. It's a grueling thing to see a young lady make a bad decision, to see that she could reverse it, and then to see her follow her own path any way. It's literally heartbreaking for parents, pastors, friends, and family.

Everyone can see the problematic results looming on the horizon—everyone except for the "decider!" Yet, they are all powerless. Parents and pastors can't force someone back through the window. Most often they try to persuade, they pray, and then they just hope for the best. They are powerless to do anything else. It's the most helpless feeling that anyone in authority can ever experience.

Here's my question. Are there godly authorities in your life that are peering through the window at you? Are they standing there praying, begging, pleading, hoping that you will turn back before it's too late? Have you made a decision that is still reversible?

If you have, I would beg you to stop in your tracks. Take off the dirty lenses that are blinding you to the dangers ahead. See the situation through the eyes of God and turn back quickly before the window closes and the long-term effects of your decision become irreversible! Make your heart right with God and come back to Him quickly while there is still time to minimize the damage that you have done to your future.

Swallow your pride! It's not worth the price you are going to pay. See the danger ahead before it's too late to turn back. God's grace is open to you, His arms are waiting to welcome you back, and a host of godly counselors will probably weep tears of joy at your return.

There's an even more important Bible principle that you need to know about. It's called the "mercy" or the "forbearance" or the "longsuffering" of God. He says in Romans 2:4, *"Or despisest thou the riches of his goodness and forbearance and longsuffering; not knowing that the goodness of God leadeth thee to repentance?"*

For all of our bad decisions, God has an eternal "window of repentance" that is always open thanks to the Cross of Calvary and the blood of Jesus Christ. Though there may be some lingering effects and scars of your bad decisions, you can always return to God in repentance. No matter where your bad decisions take you, your Heavenly Father is always pursuing, always waiting, and ever watching for your return. He stands with open arms to forgive you, to welcome you, and to restore you into His perfect plan for the rest of your life.

You cannot get so far from Him that He will not welcome you back. You cannot sin so much that He will not forgive and cleanse you. You cannot be separated from His love and grace, no matter what you've done or become. There is no power on earth that can change His feelings for you. Because of the Cross, you can step through the window of repentance at any time!

There's no doubt about it—bad decisions happen in everyone's life. We all have our "pet chicken" stories! We're all human, and we all fail. So, regardless of where you are on the "road map" of God's will...choose to be a "come-back-kid!" Follow the example of the Apostle Paul in "forgetting those things which are behind." Regardless of the mistakes you've made, God's perfect will is waiting for you...starting today!

"And the word of the LORD came unto Jonah the second time..."—Jonah 3:1a

"He saith to him again the second time, Simon, son of Jonas, lovest thou me?"—John 21:16a

Discussion Questions

1. When does God's perfect will start?
2. How does God deal with your bad decisions?
3. What is the "window of reversal"?
4. What sin can keep you from reversing your bad decisions?
5. How can your past mistakes help you in the future?
6. List three "bad decisions" that cannot be undone and explain why it is crucial to seek out God's perfect will, even after these decisions are made.
7. Why is it dangerous to dwell on past mistakes?
8. Choose two characters in the Bible who made bad decisions. Explain how their bad decisions hurt them but also how God was able to use them after they turned back to Him.

Memory Verse

"Brethren, I count not myself to have apprehended: but this one thing I do, forgetting those things which are behind, and reaching forth unto those things which are before, I press toward the mark for the prize of the high calling of God in Christ Jesus."—Philippians 3:13–14

Lesson Notes

_____

_____

_____

_____

_____

_____

_____

_____

_____

_____

_____

_____

_____

_____

_____

_____

_____

_____

_____

_____

_____

_____

_____

Hey, Dad, What's Tomorrow?

Understanding God's Call on Every Believer

Text

"Who hath saved us, and called us with an holy calling, not according to our works, but according to his own purpose and grace, which was given us in Christ Jesus before the world began,"—2 Timothy 1:9

"But as he which hath called you is holy, so be ye holy in all manner of conversation;"—1 Peter 1:15

"But ye are a chosen generation, a royal priesthood, an holy nation, a peculiar people; that ye should shew forth the praises of him who hath called you out of darkness into his marvellous light:"—1 Peter 2:9

"But as God hath distributed to every man, as the Lord hath called every one, so let him walk. And so ordain I in all churches."—1 Corinthians 7:17

"That ye would walk worthy of God, who hath called you unto his kingdom and glory."—1 Thessalonians 2:12

"Fight the good fight of faith, lay hold on eternal life, whereunto thou art also called, and hast professed a good profession before many witnesses."—1 Timothy 6:12

"But as it is written, Eye hath not seen, nor ear heard, neither have entered into the heart of man, the things which God hath prepared for them that love him."—1 Corinthians 2:9

Lesson Aim

This lesson is designed to help students understand God's call on every believer. Regardless of what a Christian does for a living, every Christian is called to live for God and to surrender their whole life for his purposes. This lesson will challenge your students to consider a call to ministry, but more importantly to surrender to God's call to live for Christ alone.

Teaching Outline

    I. First things first. (1 Peter 2:9, 21; Romans 1:6–7; Romans 8:28; Romans 8:30; 1 Corinthians 1:9; Ephesians 4:1)

        A. You are called to live for God.

        B. You are called to serve God regardless of your vocation.

        C. Full surrender to God is our reasonable service. (Romans 12:1–2)

    II. Is God calling you into ministry?

        A. A ministry call is not always a momentous experience.

        B. A ministry call is often a process of growth and realization as you follow God.

        C. God accepts volunteers into His service.

    III. There's no place like God's will.

        A. Serving in full-time ministry often gets a bad rap.

        B. Serving in full-time ministry deserves the same consideration as any other vocation.

        C. Let God be God, and you will never regret following Him. (Romans 8:15)

seventeen

Chapter Seventeen
Hey, Dad, What's Tomorrow?
Understanding God's Call on Every Believer

I often meet young adults wrestling with these and similar questions. Am I called into ministry? How will I know? What if I am and don't know it? What if I'm not and I try to go into ministry? On and on these questions could go; and the longer you consider them, the more circular the process becomes.

As we come to the end of our lessons, I want to finish up with some thoughts about your life's calling—another way of referring to destiny.

I. First things first

Whether you realize it or not…you *are* called. True, you may not be called into full-time Christian ministry, but you are still called. You are called to God. If you have trusted Jesus Christ as your Saviour, then you have been bought by His blood, redeemed by His grace, and enlisted into His cause. You are called to Him, to His purposes, and to His control—regardless of what you do for a living.

I meet a lot of young Christians who seem to draw a line of separation between those who serve in ministry and those who don't—as if there is a lesser commitment required "if I'm not called into the ministry." This is just not the case. God has placed the same call upon the life of every one of His children, regardless of where their "paycheck" comes from. Here's how God says it:

*"Who hath saved us, and **called us with an holy calling**, not according to our works, but according to his own purpose and grace, which was given us in Christ Jesus before the world began,"*—2 Timothy 1:9

*"But as he which **hath called you** is holy, so be ye holy in all manner of conversation;"*—1 Peter 1:15

*"But ye are a chosen generation, a royal priesthood, an holy nation, a peculiar people; that ye should shew forth the praises of him **who hath called you** out of darkness into his marvelous light:"*—1 Peter 2:9

*"For even hereunto **were ye called**: because Christ also suffered for us, leaving us an example, that ye should follow his steps:"*—1 Peter 2:21

*"Among whom are **ye also the called of Jesus Christ**: To all that be in Rome, beloved of God, **called to be saints**: Grace to you and peace from God our Father, and the Lord Jesus Christ."*—Romans 1:6–7

*"And we know that all things work together for good to them that love God, to them who are the **called according to his purpose**."*—Romans 8:28

*"Moreover whom he did predestinate, **them he also called**: and whom he called, them he also justified: and whom he justified, them he also glorified."*—Romans 8:30

*"God is faithful, by whom **ye were called** unto the fellowship of his Son Jesus Christ our Lord."*—1 Corinthians 1:9

*"But as God hath distributed to every man, as the **Lord hath called every one**, so let him walk…"*—1 Corinthians 7:17A

*"I therefore, the prisoner of the Lord, beseech you that ye walk worthy of the vocation **wherewith ye are called**,"* —Ephesians 4:1

*"That ye would walk worthy of God, **who hath called you** unto his kingdom and glory."*—1 Thessalonians 2:12

*"Fight the good fight of faith, lay hold on eternal life, **whereunto thou art also called**, and hast professed a good profession before many witnesses."*—1 Timothy 6:12

There's something very important to know about most of the above verses. The Holy Spirit wrote them to regular Christians. These verses were written to normal lay people like the ushers in your church or the teachers in your Sunday school. Every one of these verses makes it clear that with our salvation came the call of God upon each of our lives.

So, if you asked me, "Am I called to serve God with my life?" The biblical answer is absolutely YES! Without hesitation, you need to recognize that God wants you to serve Him with your whole heart and soul for the rest of your life. Aside from the question of whether you should enter full-time ministry, you should first commit yourself to the clear call that God has placed on the life of every believer.

In answer to this call, you should commit yourself to a lifetime of faithful service to Jesus Christ. There should be a foundational commitment in your life that no matter where you go or what you do, God will be the "center" of your life! Everything should flow from Him and ultimately be turned back towards Him for His glory. Seems extreme? Not at all! In light of the Cross of Jesus Christ, it's just our reasonable service (Romans 12:1–2).

The question of church attendance, tithing, ministry service, sharing the gospel with others, and personally walking with God should never come up in your heart. These are the non-negotiables! These are the things that *must be*, regardless of where life takes you. Regardless of the career you choose or the opportunities you seek, these foundational commitments should remain steadfast and unmovable.

II. Is God calling you into ministry?

Understanding God's call to full-time ministry is actually pretty simple if you've followed the principles that are outlined in the previous lessons. Simply put, as you yield your life completely to God, He will make it abundantly clear what you should do and when.

It's really not a formula or a predictable experience. God's "call into ministry" happens differently for various people. For me, it was more of a strong desire that I believed was my own. For others, it's more of a momentous occasion when God strongly urges them. For yet others, it's a gradual transformation of desires from within.

For example, over the years I've known many young people who didn't feel "called" into ministry, but they did feel called to God. Over time, the Lord worked new desires into their lives that gradually began to compel them into full-time ministry. Sometimes this process happens over months or even years.

The point is don't try to conjure up some momentous "call" and don't think that because lightning hasn't struck your heart, you're off the hook. It's not a hook to begin with.

Sometimes it's the decision of a moment, other times it's a process of growth, and often times, God doesn't lead His children into full-time ministry at all. Often times, He calls His children to be His strategic ambassadors to the business world, the medical world, the legal world, the construction world...and on and on it goes. Often times He chooses to provide His children with abundant financial resources through a secular career so that the cause of Christ can be funded and furthered. Whatever the case, God will place you exactly where He wants you, and in that place, you will be fulfilling the divine call of God upon your life!

III. There's no place like God's will

There truly is no place like the will of God! There's no place like being right with God, serving Him with your life, and following Him step by step. And if God would allow you to serve Him in ministry, there's no place like serving God full-time either!

I believe in the minds of some young adults, and even some older Christians, ministry gets a bad rap. Some people believe that if you surrender to ministry that means you're destined to live in poverty and suffer rejection your whole life. Some people believe that ministry requires less education or preparation than other careers. Some believe that a life in ministry is a "free-loading" lifestyle that lives off of the generosity of others. Others feel that ministry is limiting to your "true career potential." Blah, Blah, Blah. To all of these beliefs I would simply say, "Not true, not true, not true!" Every one of these assumptions is founded upon humanistic, secular thinking—which has no place in the heart of the Christian.

This lesson series has not been written to coax you in one direction over another; it has been written to bring you in line with God's will and purpose for your individual life. Yet, with any hint of the mindsets mentioned above, you're not playing on a level field. In other words, if you have deliberate, unfounded reservations against ministry or against any specific future, you're not being fair with God.

So rather than try to coax you into ministry, I would simply say to you, "Level the playing field." Give ministry the same fair consideration and prayer that you would any other direction. Give God a chance to touch your heart in that area...what are you afraid of?

Having spent the bulk of my time in or around ministry since I was eight years old, I can honestly say that serving God with your life is one of the happiest and greatest investments you could make. It's awesome and the blessings are new every day!

So, whether lightning strikes or not, just remember that you *are called*. You are called to be a faithful ambassador for the King of Kings. Answer that call, and at all costs, live out God's call upon your life one day at a time and don't let the potential of a "ministry call" spook you out. And, whatever you do, don't conjure one up. Just be content to be "called to God" and let God work out the details from there. Everything else will fall right into place.

As you pillow your head tonight, can you rest in knowing that your life is safe and secure within the Almighty hands of God? Are you fully surrendered to His will and resting upon His promises. Can you say, "God, what's tomorrow?" and be okay with any answer? If you can, then you get to be a "kid" the rest of your life! And you've got the best Dad that any kid ever had, because He really is in total control of tomorrow!

"For ye have not received the spirit of bondage again to fear; but ye have received the Spirit of adoption, whereby we cry, **Abba***, Father."*—Romans 8:15

That word *Abba*…that's a great word.
It just means "Dad."

"…as the Lord hath called every one, so let him walk." —1 Corinthians 7:17b

Discussion Questions

1. Whether or not you're called to full-time ministry, what is every Christian called to do?
2. What is your "reasonable service" to God?
3. What process is often involved in God's calling to ministry?
4. What kind of consideration should be given to full-time ministry?
5. List some basic ways that every Christian can serve God.
6. In what areas of your "reasonable service" to God do you need to grow the most in? What can you do to improve in these areas?
7. What are some false ideas people get about full-time ministry?
8. How can you let God be God in your life?

Memory Verse

"I beseech you therefore, brethren, by the mercies of God, that ye present your bodies a living sacrifice, holy, acceptable unto God, which is your reasonable service. And be not conformed to this world: but be ye transformed by the renewing of your mind, that ye may prove what is that good, and acceptable, and perfect, will of God."—Romans 12:1–2

Lesson Notes

Lesson Notes

_____

_____

_____

_____

_____

_____

_____

_____

_____

_____

_____

_____

_____

_____

_____

_____

_____

_____

_____

_____

_____

_____

_____

_____

Striving Together
P u b l i c a t i o n s

For additional Christian
growth resources visit
www.strivingtogether.com